Cultivating Emotional Intelligence

Cultivating Emotional Intelligence

The 5 Habits of the Emotion Coach

Michael G. Hylen, PhD

ROWMAN & LITTLEFIELD
Lanham • Boulder • New York • London

Published by Rowman & Littlefield
An imprint of The Rowman & Littlefield Publishing Group, Inc.
4501 Forbes Boulevard, Suite 200, Lanham, Maryland 20706
www.rowman.com

86-90 Paul Street, London EC2A 4NE, United Kingdom

British Library Cataloguing in Publication Information Available

Library of Congress Cataloging-in-Publication Data

Names: Hylen, Michael G., 1961– author.
Title: Cultivating emotional intelligence: the 5 habits of the emotion coach / Michael G. Hylen.
Description: Lanham, Maryland: Rowman & Littlefield, 2022. | Includes bibliographical references. | Summary: "Cultivating Emotional Intelligence investigates social-emotional learning, the role of teachers and school staff in cultivating student emotional intelligence, and the five elements of effective emotion coaching. The main focus of this book is the relationship between growing student emotional intelligence and teaching positive social skills"—Provided by publisher.
Identifiers: LCCN 2021035478 (print) | LCCN 2021035479 (ebook) | ISBN 9781475863000 (cloth) | ISBN 9781475863017 (paperback) | ISBN 9781475863024 (epub)
Subjects: LCSH: Affective education. | Emotions in children. | Social skills—Study and teaching.
Classification: LCC LB1072 .H95 2022 (print) | LCC LB1072 (ebook) | DDC 370.15/34—dc23
LC record available at https://lccn.loc.gov/2021035478
LC ebook record available at https://lccn.loc.gov/2021035479

This book is dedicated to my wife and children, for their sacrifice and support. To my wife, I owe more than words can express. She has been a steadfast companion and constant source of encouragement. It was she, who years ago first introduced me to the work of John Gottman. Throughout this project, as in our marriage, she has consistently believed in me. She is a source of strength and peace. It is also dedicated to my children, Michaela, Lacey, Anna Marie, Elise, Aidan, and Gabriella. Through the years of laughter, joy, tears, stress, and other feelings, you have taught me more about emotions and understanding people than I could ever teach you. I am forever grateful to be your dad and blessed by your continued love and support.

Contents

Preface

I have often heard; life is a journey. It is through this lifelong journey that we come to understand differences in people, where we fit in, and how we can make a difference. In fact, during my lifetime, I have found myself on many journeys, often overlapping. For example, I have been on a journey as a husband, at the same time a parent, a teacher, and later a principal. The information and stories shared within this book are the result of one such intersection, during my life journeys. I encountered this crossroads in the fall of 2001, when I was serving as a high school principal. The first as a high school principal, and the second as a father.

It was during this time that I was introduced to Dr. Marvin Berkowitz at the Center for Character and Citizenship. A principal colleague of mine, familiar with my work in alternative education, recommended I get to know him and his work in Character Education. After meeting Dr. Berkowitz, it was clear to me that the answers to some of the questions I had asked had nothing to do with simply getting students to obey the rules. It meant really being intentional with our school practices.

Upon realizing this, I had one more question to address, "Do school disciplinary systems really get at the root causes of problem behaviors?" Developing a comprehensive character education focused on teaching positive social skills was the starting point. But, more was needed to address the emotional struggles of many of our students—the heart of the matter. We needed to develop a comprehensive approach that embedded initiatives which focused on developing positive character traits in our students while helping them grow emotionally intelligent. We wanted to get to the root causes of the students' disruptive behaviors.

That is when my journey as a principal intersected with that of a father. I was introduced to Dr. John Gottman, not the man himself, but his book;

Raising an Emotionally Intelligent Child: The Heart of Parenting. I remember turning to my wife and saying, "That's it! This is the other component of what we should be doing in schools." In fact, this book is simply a matter of applying what I read in his book for parents to the work of teachers in schools. I discuss this a little more in detail in chapter 1. Suffice it to say, it had a profound impact on how I viewed the behaviors of my students.

As such, in addition to developing a comprehensive character education program, we began the process of incorporating Dr. Gottman's recommendations to parents into our work as educators. We focused our energy on becoming emotion coaches. For many of the teachers in the school, it was easy to become an excellent emotion coach. While it did not eliminate problem behaviors in the school, the positive impact it had on reducing repeat problem behaviors by students and a positive impact on school climate was noticeable.

Eventually, I began presenting this approach at conferences and as professional development. At one such conference, a superintendent asked me if I had written a book on the content and if it was available to use with teachers during professional development. At that time, there was nothing specifically available to educators about applying emotion coaching in schools. Dr. Gottman's work was specifically written for parents for use in the home.

I reached out to Dr. Gottman at the Gottman Institute via email about the possibility of my writing one. He replied with great enthusiasm that I should do so. After many years of writing and rewriting, this book represents the finished product of that effort. While the foundation of this book lies in Dr. Gottman's, as well as Dr. Berkowitz's work as you will see, it is quite different in scope. I hope you find it as stimulating of thought as did theirs.

Acknowledgments

Where to begin? Simply put, none of this work would have been possible if not for the teachers and students I have been blessed to work with. Their willingness to share their stories and life journeys played an integral role in this work. They may never know how much they enriched my life as an educator and father.

I am very thankful to have crossed paths with Kira Hall at Rowman & Littlefield. I can honestly say that her patience and support through the publication process were invaluable to this book becoming a reality. I want to thank Dr. Tom Koerner and the dedicated team at Rowman & Littlefield for believing in this project and for the support of educators everywhere.

Finally, I would be amiss if I did not thank my sister, Kathleen Hylen. Her diligence, patience, and support provided thorough feedback and insight that is not served justice by simple words. Her open and honest feedback was vital to the flow and readability of this work. To say the least, I greatly value your love and support.

Chapter 1

Introduction

ABOUT THE BOOK

Sometimes students make mistakes with their behavioral choices. If we are honest with ourselves, we all do. When it is brought to their attention, there is often a progression of emotions they endure. At first, they may be ashamed. Shame then may morph into fear. They are afraid of what the ramifications of their actions may be. And, in some cases, they feel alone. In school, it becomes up to the teacher to walk them through these times and the emotions they are experiencing. The process of doing so is the focus of this book.

This book is, first and foremost, about relationships and understanding oneself and others. Human beings are designed for relationships. Much of the key work of the positive psychology movement in the 1990s supports the benefits of interacting with others and staying positive. Additionally, research findings in the field of neurobiology reflect the importance of social attachments in the early years of child development and the impact such attachments have on the development of the brain's systems underlying understanding of human social behavior (see Wismer Fries et al., 2005).

As humans, we understand the importance of developing lasting relationships. Such relationships are attained through intimacy. For the purposes of this book, intimacy occurs when we are able to know someone, and be known by them, without fear of rejection (Wagner and McGee, 2016). This is discussed further in chapter 2. We begin the intimacy process by gradually revealing important details of who we are and our passions, joys, and deep-seeded fears, while simultaneously, patiently gathering the same information about the person with whom we are bonding. When we first meet someone, we know to stand at a distance as to not "crowd personal space." Over time, we feel more comfortable standing closer. The same holds true emotionally. Initially, we keep a distance. Over time, we become more willing to reveal more personal details of ourselves, as a sign of our growing intimacy.

Yet educators are interesting beings, as teachers are often not willing to take this same approach with our students. Most often, we expect them to willingly reveal personal details of their lives to us, with a blind sense of trust, simply by nature of our position. We expect it even though students lack a real understanding of us. We fail to give our students the same patience we show in developing our relationships with those who become trusted friends. Yet, we expect the same return in value from our students as if we were a trusted friend without developing the relationship at that level. When this occurs, it is a result of failing to recognize the human nature of students in regard to developing trusting relationships.

The hope is that as the teacher begins incorporating the five habits of *Emotion Coaching* detailed in this book, the process will naturally entail intimacy-building processes. While the ultimate goal of the process is helping students develop emotional intelligence, the hope exists that the teacher will reap the benefits as well. Such benefits may include more positive teacher-student interactions, a growth in positive student behaviors in the classroom, and a more positive classroom/school climate.

The second thing this book sets out to do is remind us that, as teachers, we come to our classrooms from a broad framework. Teachers enter their classrooms with more than just the perspective of an educator; they are family members, friends, and colleagues as well. As such, much of what we understand about students and their behaviors comes from experiences beyond the classroom. Some of our personal viewpoints come as a result of experiences encountered as family members, parents, and friends.

As we seek to better understand relational skills from that of a parent or friend, we indirectly grow in our understanding of our students. For example, a teacher who is a parent of a young child may seek to find positive means for disciplining their child when they misbehave. During the process, they come to see how such an approach may be applied with their students. The same can be said regarding growing emotionally intelligent children as can be said of students.

The challenge in this case is for teachers who work with older students who have not been given the appropriate attention to such matters as a young child. Such cases have been observed in upper elementary, middle school, and high school students. In these situations, the teacher is challenged with addressing the student in an age-appropriate manner while redirecting him or her as if he or she were a younger child. The material in this book is presented in a manner such that teachers may adapt it to their setting and student needs as they see appropriate.

Ultimately, this book is designed to help the teacher gain a greater appreciation of the power a trusting relationship can have on the development of a student's social-emotional intelligence. In addition, the hope is that you will come to see the important role conversation and empathy play in helping students understand themselves and develop positive social skills. Too often schools rely on the application of rules and codes of conduct systems for managing student behaviors without considering the impact on their emotional intelligence development. By incorporating the habits presented in this book into the "modus operandi," more emphasis is given on helping the student grow emotionally, not just behaviorally.

This work finds its roots in John Gottman's work *Raising an Emotionally Intelligent Child: The Heart of Parenting.* Through reading this book and attending various workshops, it was easy to see how this approach to raising emotionally intelligent children could easily be applied in schools. It was encouraging to think of how the process could be applied to teaching student's positive social skills. Even more encouraging was to consider how the role it could play in addressing student problem behaviors with more long-term goals in mind. When it comes to student development, more is at stake than just academics and learning to follow the rules.

Throughout history, education has had two great goals: to help people become smart and to help them become good (Lickona, 1991). However, in today's society, these two goals have become somewhat skewed. The first goal has remained basically the same—to provide a climate for student learning and academic achievement. But, the second has been altered. Public education tends to focus more on simply reducing student problem behavior instead of developing positive character traits and growing emotionally intelligent students.

What difference does it make? Can it not be asked: "Through the process of teaching right and wrong behaviors, are we not teaching positive character traits?" In some cases, yes. In others, not necessarily. When schools focus on behavior, often the notions of right and wrong are the concern. A focus on ethics is certainly something schools should be encouraged to do. However, when a school concentrates on building positive character, the focus shifts to acts of virtue (e.g., kindness, integrity, and empathy). Instruction on both ethics and virtues is needed. The problem is that schools tend to focus on the ethics and behaviors piece to the exclusion of teaching and practicing virtuous character traits. The impact is being felt in the classroom and society alike.

Without an intentional focus on replacing those behaviors with appropriate character traits, schools will fall short in their efforts to "produce good citizens." And, while character education efforts provide a solid groundwork for doing so, additional strategies must be explored for addressing unwanted and negative student behaviors. Such interventions can result in the positive growth of student social skills. This is especially true when serving students with emotional and behavioral challenges.

The question schools must begin to address is: How are such phrases as "productive" or "good" citizens defined? For example, one could demonstrate that a good citizen is a person who acts responsibly in their community, pays their taxes, is a law-abiding citizen, and even pitches in during a time of crisis. This type of citizen is the one who demonstrates good character through giving to local charities. Certainly, schools would want this of their graduates.

On the other hand, should schools seek to set higher expectations of their graduates? For example, could we seek to produce citizens that are more active in their communities? Ones who not only participate in community efforts but also take leadership roles in them. Citizens who understand how to plan for the success of collective tasks. Citizens who understand how government agencies work and strive to improve their community. Citizens who not only give to local charities but also help organize their efforts in meeting their client's needs.

Alternatively, should schools seek to take it even one step further? Should we seek to produce citizens who are capable of critically assessing the political, economic, social, and cultural structures of not only their local communities but also the greater community at-large? Such citizens play an active role in seeking to eliminate the root causes that lead to people's need for the support of local charities. Such citizens understand social injustice and seek to effect change. Citizens at this level have the ability to understand community issues beyond what is apparent on the surface level.

The core assumptions schools must address about developing students into "good" and "productive" citizens must be reevaluated. Is it enough to produce citizens who have good character, who are honest, responsible, law-abiding citizens? Or, do we seek something more? To produce citizens who not only manifest such traits but also go further by actively taking leadership roles within community structures for the sake of improving conditions for its members. Even more so, should schools seek to produce citizens who go even one step further by seeking to solve societal problems through questioning and challenging established structures that lead to inherent injustices?

This book itself does not delve that deeply into the construct of developing "good" or "productive" citizens. It does, however, seek to challenge educators to consider more deeply terminology and practices used in the development of their students. Specifically, as it pertains to the growth and development of student emotional intelligence and character traits.

THE JOURNEY: WHY EMOTION COACHING?

You are on a journey. A journey you say? Yes, a journey. Teaching is a journey and it is how we come to understand who we are, who our students are, and how we make a difference. In fact, teachers find themselves on many journeys in their lifetime, some simultaneous (e.g., the journey of parenthood simultaneous with the journey of classroom teaching). The material presented within this book is the result of the author's journey from a teacher, giver of knowledge to educator, to a collaborator in student growth and development. In addition, it came about because of his journey as a parent.

Two events, occurring somewhat simultaneously, played a significant role in this shift. Both events occurred outside of the schoolhouse building. The first, was being introduced to the book by John Gottman entitled *Raising an Emotionally Intelligent Child: The Heart of Parenting.* This took place at a seminar on the same topic. The book was transformative; the author did come to understand the role not only he played in the emotional development of his own children but those of his students as well. How could this information be incorporated into school efforts at growing student emotional intelligence?

The second event took place on a normal fall day. On that day, the author, a high school principal, arrived home to find his two oldest daughters (three and five years old at the time) sitting just inside the front door on the bottom steps to the second floor. They were holding hands and complimenting each other in a very pleasant manner. To say the least, this was not a common occurrence. Perplexed, he turned to his left to catch the image of his wife walking toward him with a look suggesting the dialogue between the two girls was not a volunteer activity.

Gathering from the look on his face, she knew further explanation was necessary. She informed him that the girls had been fighting with each other and that she wanted them to spend some time expressing how much they truly did appreciate one another. The question then was posed: "What would you have done?" The problem with the answer to that question was the setting. As a high school principal in a school building, the answer would have been simple. Based on the Code of Conduct book that had been developed, both girls would have been suspended for three days. That was the answer that had been set in the building.

If only life were so uncomplicated. At home, as a parent, we tend to consider things in a broader, more long-term sense. We tend to look for consequences that are not focused on punitive measures solely, but address the heart of the matter. We take time with our own children to process events and explain the consequences we are instilling for the purpose of their long-term growth. Interactions such as these often take time. Unfortunately, this is the challenge for schools, finding the time.

This was the turning point in the journey. Questions began to abound. Is this really what our discipline codes have come to, simply managing students? Is this why some students struggle with problem behaviors? Discipline codes have become so focused on consequences that they fail to have a positive impact on student social behaviors. Do school disciplinary systems really get at the heart of the matter or are they so focused on creating a safe and orderly environment that they fail to have any intrinsic value of their own? In other words, are our reactions toward student's negative expression of emotions (problem behaviors) beneficial in helping the student grow socially and emotionally? There has to be a better way.

This is not to suggest that this new direction in the journey started by getting rid of all rules or codes of conduct. After all, rules are for the purpose of establishing expectations, a good thing to do. And codes of conduct serve as a convenient means for determining consequences, affording student academic learning in the classroom or school building to get back on track quickly. But it did suggest that an evaluation needed to take place of the value of such rules and consequences in terms of student growth and development socially and emotionally. If schools are to take the social and emotional development of students seriously, in addition to the academic, then all elements of learning, both inside and outside of the classroom, must become a channel for doing so.

Another result of this shift in direction was a change in understanding of the dynamics of relational communication. Parent/teacher to child/student communication usually for this author entailed a unidirectional flow: the adult speaking and the student/child listening. While there is a place and time for such a type of communication, it poses limitations on many aspects of child's/student's development. Some of the dynamics to consider regarding unidirectional flow are as follows:

- When I was doing all the talking, it was because I often had a timeline in mind, that benefited me.
- When the student had an opportunity to speak, I was understanding and learning patience.
- When I was doing all the talking, I defined the relationship.
- When the student was afforded the opportunity to share openly, I understood them better and the relationship grew deeper.

These revelations were especially important when thinking in terms of student social-emotional growth and development. If the adult is constantly doing all the talking, especially in regard to telling the child how they should feel, the child is not being given the opportunity to express their feelings in a supportive environment. If the adult is setting time limits on growth expectations, the student can become overwhelmed and begin to lose hope. Patience on the part of the adult affords the student time to grow in a positive manner.

Like that of the author's journey, the goal of this book is to help you unpack events that played a role in your personal social-emotional growth and development. Along the way, it may possibly give you a new perspective on emotions and the negative behaviors of students. Hopefully, your perspective will see these entities as opportunities to develop more intimate (explained later) and trusting relationships with your students as you walk them through the social-emotional growth and development process.

It is also designed to help you gain a greater appreciation of the power such trusting relationships can have on the development of a student's social-emotional intelligence. The desire is that you will come to see the important role conversation and empathy play in helping students understand themselves and develop positive social skills as you help them grow their emotional intelligence. Dr. Marvin Berkowitz once shared that one of the most influential variables in human development is social relationship. This especially applies to the emotionally sustaining qualities of a relationship.

Where you are on your journey and the direction you want to head is up to you. You may start over by considering what effect the power relationships during your formative years of development had on shaping how you express yourself today. You may be a parent and teacher who is trying to reconcile how you approach your child's development and that of your students. Or, you may just be interested in working toward playing a more positive role in the emotional development of your students.

Regardless of where we are on our personal journey, it is at a key moment in time for our students. Simply put, just as we are on a journey, so are our students. More than likely, their journey is toward one of belonging. More than ever, students are seeking a sense of belonging. For many, belongingness is most evident by an absence in their life, rather by its presence. For these, the journey will be long. And where they are in their social-emotional development is vital to how quickly there will be an essence of fulfillment to their sense of belonging.

This is where your journey and theirs will intersect and the challenges students face can be equally as difficult as yours. Sometimes, as teachers, we overlook this reality. With the advent of social media, the essence of childhood and youth has changed significantly over the past decade or two (Valkenburg and Piotrowski, 2017). This is especially true when considering the social-emotional development of our students. Your role in leading them in their emotional formation will be paramount. Teachers must embrace the reality that their role has expanded to include one of mentor, advisee, confidant, role model, and coach. Your ability to serve each of these roles in a positive manner will be the difference in the lives of many of your students. Moreover, your ability to serve as an *emotion coach* will be vital.

Failure Is Not an Option: It's Not Just about the Five Rs

In 1995, Universal Studios, in conjunction with Imagine Entertainment, released its blockbuster movie *Apollo 13*. The movie is based upon the real-life events surrounding the aborted Apollo 13 lunar mission in 1970. One unexpected consequence of the movie's fame was the notoriety it gained in the field of K–12 education. One simple connection to education comes from one of the more famous mantras spoken within one scene; "Failure is not an option!" Just over five years after these famous words were spoken on the big screen, educators were introduced to the No Child Left Behind Act where the message was clear, "failure is not an option."

For those unfamiliar with the movie, the background is as follows. In the specific scene in which these words are spoken, Gene Krantz (played by Ed Harris) has just been informed of the explosion aboard the Odyssey and its impending doom. Krantz has assembled all key figures (experts) into one room to discuss options for bringing the astronauts safely home. At one point in this scene, Krantz exclaims, "We have never lost an American in space and we're sure as hell not going to on my watch. And failure is not an option!" It was not long afterward that the phrase found its place in the world of education. By 2010, Alan Blankenstein had released the second edition of his book titled *Failure Is Not an Option: 6 Principles for Making Student Success the Only Option.*

Blankenstein's book addresses a number of key issues educators must consider if failure is truly not an option. Matters such as courageous leadership, *relational trust*, collaborative teaming, and family and community engagement are addressed as part of it. It is a highly recommended book and does a great job of looking at the things schools need to consider to improve student academic achievement. However, notably missing from the book is the matter of addressing student social and emotional growth.

It is well noted that student problem behavior remains one of the biggest challenges for teachers in the classroom. Its impact, in some cases a major one, on academic achievement is well documented (see Chambers et al., 2006; Hylen, 2008). Though many of today's students are well served by the principles presented by Blankenstein, students who struggle socially and emotionally, as manifested through problem behaviors, fall through the cracks. If failure is truly not an option, then education must look beyond what this book refers to as the five Rs: reading, "riting" (writing), "rithmetic," rules, and regulations. Education needs to take a more proactive approach in incorporating student development in two other important Rs—respect and responsibility.

One challenge is that student populations are becoming more heterogeneous. As the population becomes more heterogeneous, terms like respect and responsibility become more difficult to define due to the variance in each student's experience with the terms. Students within a classroom may differ substantially in their perception of, and reaction to, objective dissimilarities, such that classroom expectations may be interpreted differently by each class member, leading to different behavioral responses.

A good representation of this construct within education is found in Dr. Ruby Payne's work *A Framework for Understanding Poverty: A Cognitive Approach*. In her research, Dr. Payne (1995) discovered how the "hidden values" students of differing socioeconomic levels bring to the classroom impact their understanding of specific constructs (e.g., respect and responsibility) and thus their behaviors. Hence, hidden deep within the expectation of increased academic achievement is the need for schools to develop more productive systems for developing student social-emotional skills aimed at helping them develop a better sense of respect and responsibility from a more global perspective. We address this construct in more detail in chapter 3.

Teachers find themselves striving to resolve two conflicts simultaneously: student achievement and social-emotional growth. Yet, schools are judged on only one. However, reliance on test scores and academic measurements alone do not represent a school's true impact on its students. Still, working with students who struggle with social-emotional issues can be immensely satisfying for teachers. Despite the satisfying nature of the work, teachers in such situations may find themselves frustrated by the perceived lack of success they are having with students because of these traditional methods for measuring success and the pressure to produce high-scoring students.

One side effect of the pressure of high-stakes testing is the limitations on time teachers have to address the social-emotional growth of their students. Teachers often recognize that some students are falling short academically because of social and emotional struggles with which they are grappling, not because of intellectual inability. They recognize that changes in instructional techniques will do little help. Such teachers further recognize that schools that fail to include specific interventions aimed at assisting student growth in social-emotional maturity are bound to fail in assisting students to develop a more global sense of respect and responsibility and ultimately in finding academic success.

Can We Truly Teach Emotions and Character? Aristotle Thought So

One of the questions heard in schools whenever a discussion arises about character education initiatives is: "Why do we have to teach this stuff?" This matter is addressed later in this book. What is becoming a bigger question today is: "Can character be taught? And, can we truly teach students about their emotions?" Aristotle believed the answer was yes. To Aristotle, education had a threefold purpose: first, to develop student potential for reasoning; second, to help students learn a skill and grow their knowledge base; and third, to help students form ethical character (see educationalroots.weebly .com/Aristotle). In other words, student dispositional growth was as important as student growth in academic knowledge.

So where do emotions come into the picture? Aristotle believed that there were five distinct features to consider addressing student dispositions and character (Arthur et al., 2017). According to Arthur et al. (2017), Aristotle believed that character education efforts should focus on: (1) human flourishing (behaviors that help others flourish); (2) cultivating virtues through one's lived experiences that become habits in life over time; (3) moral dilemmas (working through issues requiring decisions to be made between right versus right instead of just wrong versus right); (4) education (teaching positive character traits from an early age); and (5) emotions.

Aristotle believed that education was for the purpose of helping students learn not just knowledge and behaviors but also about emotions. He understood how emotions drove our actions, interactions, and behaviors. This is a key point in this book. Aristotle believed that teaching students about their emotions from a young age helped them better manage and regulate them later in life. Additionally, he believed that the tie between motivation and emotions was a strong one. This is another key point discussed later in this work.

The question then is: "How can teachers teach about emotions?" Teaching about emotions is not a great challenge, growing emotionally intelligent students is. It is possible for teachers to instruct students about the concept of emotions and the varying types. Teachers are also able to help students define the varying terms. But for teachers to truly help students understand their feelings and respond well to them takes time and great effort. The emphasis here is not on the knowledge of emotions, rather an understanding of them, in terms of behaviors and positive social skills.

The focus of this book is on the latter. As you journey through this book, the hope is that you will embrace the role you play as mentor, advisee, confidant, role model, and coach. Your ability to serve each of these roles well will have a huge impact on the lives of the students entrusted into your care. And, as stated earlier, your ability to serve as an *emotion coach* will be vital.

Chapter 2

Understanding Emotional
Intelligence and Behaviors

EMOTIONAL INTELLIGENCE: WHAT IS
IT AND WHY IS IT IMPORTANT?

Before we go any further in this journey, it is important to first define the construct of emotional intelligence (EI), or what some refer to as emotional quotient (EQ). What is it? As a psychological theory, the construct of emotional intelligence was first introduced by Peter Salovey and John Mayer in 1990. Salovey began by taking a wider view of Howard Gardner's work on intelligence, specifically as it pertained to what is referred to as "personal intelligences." Gardner first introduced the idea of multiple intelligences in 1983.

In his later work, *Multiple Intelligences*, Gardner divided personal intelligence into two types: *inter*personal and *intra*personal. Briefly, he summarizes the two as,

> *Inter*personal intelligence is the ability to understand other people; what motivates them, how they work, how to work cooperatively with them. . . .
> *Intra*personal intelligence . . . is a correlative ability, turned inward. It is the capacity to form an accurate, veridical model of oneself and to be able to use that model to operate effectively in life. (p. 9)

Salovey, in his definition of emotional intelligence, expanded the abilities associated with Gardner's personal intelligences into five domains: knowing one's emotions; managing emotions; motivating oneself; recognizing the emotions in others; and, handling emotions (Goleman, 1995).

The goal of developing a strong emotional intelligence is not to change who a person is. The purpose is to help one better understand emotions and how to respond appropriately to them, to replace negative behaviors with positive ones and to have a greater awareness of others and society as a whole. It is a matter of replacing a system of thinking in terms of dos and don'ts with an understanding of emotions, specifically in light of their impact on positive social skills.

As stated earlier, Dr. Peter Salovey was one of the first to break down emotional intelligence into five realms. Building off Salovey's and others work, Daniel Goleman (1995) narrowed down the five realms into four categories: self-awareness, social awareness; self-management, and relationship management. Each of these four categories is placed into two of four quadrants on a continuum. Self-awareness and social awareness fall in the "recognition" category, with self-awareness also being classified in the "self" category while social awareness falls into the "social" category. Similarly, self-management and relationship management are classified in the "regulation" category simultaneously with being divided into self and social. The goal is to move in two directions: first, from self to the social; and second, from the recognition category to the "regulation" category: self-management and relationship management (www.accipio.com: Goleman's 5 elements).

While not everyone agrees with Goleman's model of emotional intelligence, research suggests that emotional intelligence is something that can improve over time (positivepsychology.com/emotional-intelligence-frameworks). Additionally, there is a need to understand the complexity of emotions as it pertains to reason. It is important to note that emotional states can be in harmony or out of harmony with reason and that no emotion we feel represents a judgment on a matter, rather how we feel in response to circumstances (Lewis, 1993). As such, investing time and energy into the process of developing one's own emotional intelligence and the EQ of other's becomes a worthy endeavor.

Psychology Today (www.psychologytoday.com) offers this take on EQ, "Emotional intelligence refers to the ability to identify and manage one's own emotions, as well as the emotions of others." *The School of Life* (www.theschooloflife.com) presents another variation on the definition. They state: "Emotional Intelligence is the quality that enables us to confront with patience, insight and imagination the many problems that we face in our affective relationship with ourselves and with other people." Think of it this way, emotional intelligence is the way we behave in response to the emotions we feel as well as how we respond to the way others display emotions.

Have you ever asked yourself "why do I act this way" or "why should I care"? Or, have you ever heard a student state "I don't know what's wrong with me." Have you wondered if there is something wrong with you or someone else because they get angry over the simplest things? How you answer these questions is a reflection of your emotional intelligence or EQ.

Recognizing and responding appropriately to the emotions we feel is a demonstration of a well-developed EQ.

Now consider your thoughts and feelings when observing students and others as they display their emotions or express negative feelings. What are your initial thoughts? What is your initial response? Again, the way we think and act during such times is another reflection of our EQ. As was the case with understanding our own emotional responses, our ability to recognize and respond appropriately to the emotions and behaviors of others is a demonstration of a well-developed EQ.

One thing to make note of here is the use of the term "response." People with a strong EQ are more apt to "respond" to others rather than "react." What is the difference? Referring back to *Psychology Today* (September, 2016),

A reaction is survival oriented and on some level a defense mechanism. It might turn out okay but is often something you regret later. A response on the other hand usually comes more slowly. It's based on both the conscious and unconscious mind.

In other words, how we act in regard to a student's display of negative or positive emotions represents our development on the emotional intelligence continuum.

It can be said that emotional intelligence is the ability to respond well to challenges presented by both negative and positive emotions. These challenges may be internal, the emotions we feel personally, or external, the emotions and behaviors demonstrated by others. Either way, it is our response or reaction to such stimuli that serves as a measurement of our EQ. In social life, the level of development of our emotional intelligence is reflected through how we conduct ourselves personally and how sensitive we are to the moods of others, regardless of our personal motivations.

Hopefully, this gives a glimpse into why having a strong EQ is important. Consider the following scenario: you witness an interaction between a teenage male student and his high school principal. The student had come to the principal's office after just having punched a wall in the school hallway. His hand was badly hurt, and the wall had a big hole in it. Given that he had punched a wall and there was no specific "rule" about not doing so, the principal asked the student if he understood why he had been sent to his office. His response might surprise some; he simply stated, "Yes, because I got angry."

His response is a clear representation of his emotional intelligence developmental level at the time. During his formative years, adult reactions and responses to inappropriate behaviors he displayed had led him to believe that getting angry was the problem. In other words, the emotion he experienced internally was the problem, not the outward manifestation of it, the punching.

What was clear was that his emotional intelligence was not developing in a positive manner. One can imagine the young man repeatedly exhausting himself trying to find a way to not get angry rather than finding positive alternatives to expressing his anger.

The aforementioned example points to an important student need—social-emotional learning opportunities. Too often student emotional intelligence development occurs through the application of rules and codes of conduct systems. Yet, three inherent flaws with such an approach are evident. The first one is that established "rules" often make the assumption that by telling a student what not to do, that they will know what to do (Vincent, 2005). The second is that student problem behaviors occur in a vacuum, void of any emotion. And, the third is that positive behaviors are best taught by declaring moral actions as simply following the rules rather than being socially aware and having strong relationship management skills (e.g. Rule #1—"Don't talk when someone else is talking" instead of "It is important to listen to others and hear what they have to say").

Let's talk more about point #2, regarding emotional intelligence development; problem behaviors, and positive ones as well, do not occur in a vacuum. In the previous example, the young man's inappropriate behavior was the direct response to an emotion of anger. However, processes used to address his behaviors never dealt directly with helping him understand and address anger in a positive manner. He had never been taught how to understand emotions and how to respond to them in a positive manner. His only known reactions were negative by nature and resultant consequences focused solely on the behaviors. As such, he came to see negative emotions themselves as the problem.

One factor to consider in the matter of student emotional intelligence is that today's student populations often have fewer family supports in their homes and are more heavily involved with social media. Hence, emotional reactions are not readily monitored, and emotional intelligence is not cultivated in a positive manner. While the impact of fewer family supports on student behavior is readily understood, we are only now getting a full understanding of the impact of social media on a person's EQ. Even so, some educators still question the need for social-emotional learning in the classroom and developing student EQ.

This hesitancy on behalf of teachers may be due to the reality that educators have to strive to resolve two conflicts simultaneously, student academic achievement and social-emotional wellness, where there appears to be a greater emphasis placed on the former. Hence, developing student emotional intelligence is not something addressed in many schools. Yet, working with students who struggle with social-emotional issues can be immensely satisfying for teachers despite the pressure placed on them to produce high-scoring students.

If educators are going to nurture the positive development of students' emotional intelligence and social skills, it will be necessary to reframe traditional practices that focus on promoting positive behaviors through a system of rules and regulations. Teaching positive social skills can be a complex matter in schools that fail to address the emotional well-being of its students and fail to recognize the power of building relationships as part of the developmental process. Emotional intelligence is not something that can be taught through a course in school. As such, schools that lack a personal approach to helping its students mature in emotional intelligence fail to prepare its most at-risk students for future success.

The Impact Parents, Teachers, and Other Adults Have on Our EQ Development

Hopefully, you now have a deeper understanding of what emotional intelligence is. The time has come to delve a little into how it is developed within us. Remember, student emotional intelligence is not something taught in a class at school. So then, where and how is our EQ developed? The answer to the first part of the question is simple: mostly in the home and somewhat from our communities. Most of our EQ development stems from how our parents, or significant adults in our life, expressed their emotions and how and to what extent they allowed us to do so.

One of the most influential variables in human development is social relationships (Berkowitz, 2012b). Research findings from the neurobiological field reflect the importance of social attachments in the early years of child development and its impact on the development of the brain systems underlying basic aspects of human social behavior (Fries et al., 2005). In addition, research indicates that students long for caring relationships with adults (Chambers et al., 2005). Research from the field of psychology supports these findings. According to Kathryn Whitted (2011), research has substantiated the importance of fostering positive relationships between children and their caregivers during infancy and early childhood (p. 11).

Child developmental theorists believe that positive relationships with primary caregivers are critical to our social and emotional developmental needs (Whitted, 2011). The definition of neglect includes "the failure to provide the emotional nurturing necessary" (www.safechild.org). Have you ever asked yourself, "How did my parents/adults express their emotions? Did they ignore them from what you could tell? Did they lash out? Did they express their feelings in a safe manner?" Or, have you ever considered the question, "Were you allowed to express your emotions openly?" If so, how did your parents and others respond to you when you did? A lot about us in terms of our EQ is revealed by how a conflict was handled and the type of comfort, or lack thereof, we received at a time of heightened emotions when we were growing up.

Of course, the answers to the aforementioned questions may vary depending upon which parent or adult we are referring to at the time. It is not uncommon to hear how one parent was very expressive while the other "held things in." And in most cases, when emotions were being expressed openly, rarely were they expressed in a manner considered safe. Furthermore, the manner in which we respond to our emotions is not solely set by the examples we witnessed during our formative years.

There is a second set of questions to be considered. As an adult, have you ever considered the questions, "How do I respond when a young person expresses their emotions in a negative way? Do others trust me with their expression of emotion? Are there similarities to that of how my own parents and other adults responded?" Our responses to our emotions were probably shaped by adults in our lives, whether or not the adult intended to do so. The experiences of our growing years molded our views on the importance, or lack of importance, of our feelings and those of others. Adults are role models at all times. With that said, be kind, parents and other adults are simply responding in a manner they deem appropriate based upon their EQ development constructed through the adults in their lives.

Consider the impact phrases such as "you need to get over it" or "you need to toughen up" may have on the emotional development of a child. Or, the impact a question such as "Oh, did you get your feelings hurt?" may have. Add to the matter that such phrases are not limited in scope of use by parents, but are sentiments commonly shared by coaches, teachers, peers, and friends. For many people, especially of particular generations, these responses are a natural reaction because it was how we were taught by the many different people in our lives to deal with our emotions.

Nonetheless, the results of this type of upbringing have important implications for both childhood and adulthood. First, many young people grow up learning to restrain displays of emotions. As a result, they pay the physical, emotional, and social toll for such. Or, they learn to express them in a manner that is not positive and bear the negative consequences of this behavior. Second, an upbringing that fails to instill positive ways of understanding and expressing emotions leads adults to struggle with helping others express their emotions appropriately.

Let's refer to the example given earlier of the young man who looked to punch things whenever he got angry. One could deduce that during his childhood, it was not uncommon for him to observe a parent who, whenever angry, responded with some type of aggressive behavior. As he was in the formative years of his EQ development, he came to see this type of behavior as an appropriate response when angry or frustrated. The fact was that he had never been provided an opportunity to express negative emotions in a positive manner. Whenever he wanted to share his feelings of anger, he was informed he needed to control his anger or that he simply needed to "get over it." Such responses, while not meant to be harmful, stunted his EQ development and simply left him only understanding one way in which to manifest anger and frustration.

Similar to his experiences at home, he found himself equally frustrated with the manner with which his behaviors were addressed at school. One reason for this is that the process most schools use to address inappropriate student behavior is rigid. One of the biggest drawbacks of this structure is that discipline simply becomes submission to the rules. Many of today's codes of conduct have become so focused on creating a safe and orderly environment that they cease to have any intrinsic learning value of their own (Hylen, 2008). Very little opportunity is given in these structured systems to allow for the adult to help the student process their emotions in a safe manner. As such, student emotional intelligence is not developed in a positive manner.

If educators are to take seriously the EQ development of students as a component of improving positive interpersonal skills, all components of the educational program should become a conduit for such instruction (Berkowitz, 2012b). The assumption that positive behaviors are best taught by declaring rules by which to live rather than establishing, teaching, and practicing positive normative social skills has long had a negative impact on the emotional intelligence development of young people.

Still, many schools incorporate behavior modification techniques into their daily routine. Behavior modification approaches make one basic assumption: people's behaviors are largely the result of experiences with environmental stimuli (Skinner, 1971). Skinner referred to these phenomena as *conditioning*. School discipline programs seek to use conditioning to decrease and eliminate undesirable behaviors based upon punishment but fail to equip the student with a more appropriate response (Ormrod, 2003). As such, extrinsic motivators, such as loss of recess, rather than intrinsic motivators, such as seeking to do right, impact student classroom behavior more readily but fail to eliminate student problem behavior because they do not address emotions.

The contention here is that adults should reframe the manner in which they think about rules and consequences as the best means of addressing problem behaviors. It is a matter of changing from viewing rules, dos and don'ts behaviors, as the best means of teaching students to act positively, to a focus on developing a process by which students can learn to express emotions in a safe manner and develop positive social skills through it. This is not to suggest that rules and consequences are bad. The point here is to dispel a common belief that implementing a system of established rules with clearly defined consequences in and of themselves, without addressing student EQ growth and development, help students develop positive social skills.

The key here is to note that growing emotionally intelligent children does not mean the end to discipline (Gottman, 1997, p. 27). Rather growing emotionally intelligent students means that they better understand their actions and resulting consequences. Students with a high EQ understand when they have acted inappropriately and most often expect consequences as a result. Even so, it is imperative that the consequences levied against the student be logical to the consequence with correction as the point of emphasis, not punishment. This concept will be discussed in more detail in chapter 4.

Educators across the nation are talking about the need to infuse social-emotional learning into their school programs. Rightfully so, it is a key element missing from the work many schools are doing with their student body. As teachers, we share a common understanding that such efforts will have a positive impact on a school's climate and culture. We also know the important role parents play in the growth and development of their child's emotional intelligence. Unfortunately, the reality is that many students attending schools and alternative programs across the nation come from homes where parents do not specifically address the topic in the house for a variety of reasons.

The reality exists that if the adults in a student's life do not address social-emotional learning in a positive manner, the likelihood that society will address it when it is too late, will dramatically increase. Educators who work with at-risk student populations will agree that the role they play in helping students find a better path than the one they are on is critical. These teachers point out how often students look to them for support, encouragement, and direction because it is lacking at home. As a result, educators find themselves striving to resolve two conflicts simultaneously, student achievement and social-emotional issues. Hence, reliance on test scores and measurements is not likely to yield enough data about a teacher's true impact on his or her students.

Working with students who struggle with social-emotional issues can be immensely satisfying for teachers. Yet, teachers in such situations may consistently find themselves frustrated by the perceived lack of success they are having with many students because of these traditional methods for measuring success. Compounding this frustration is the reality of the pressure placed on teachers from their superiors to produce high-scoring students.

The absence of a good measurement tool for evaluating impact is not the only thing frustrating many teachers. Often teachers working with students struggling with traditional school approaches find themselves asking, "If we are supposed to be helping students lacking success through traditional efforts, why is it we are not doing anything different?" Most often any specialized efforts designed to help students achieve fail to address the socioemotional needs that underlie the problems that lead to a student's need for added support in the first place.

Consider the case of a student who is failing academically in school due to the lack of motivation. The reality of the matter is that the student's lack of motivation may be a manifestation of social and emotional struggles with which they are grappling. Program changes in instructional techniques or settings will do little to help. Simply put, failing to include specific interventions aimed at assisting the student's positive growth in social and emotional intelligence is bound to fail in assisting with academic growth.

The impact an adult can have on the emotional development of a child is immense. This is especially true of educators. One often-used quote in the character education movement comes from Haim Ginott, an Israeli schoolteacher, a child psychologist and psychotherapist, and a parent educator. In his book *Teacher and child: A book for parents and teachers*, Ginott penned:

> I've come to the frightening conclusion that I am the decisive element in the classroom. My personal approach creates the climate. My daily mood makes the weather. As a teacher, I possess a tremendous power to make a child's life miserable or joyous. I can be a tool of torture or an instrument of inspiration. I can humiliate or humor, hurt or heal. In all situations, it is my response that decides whether a crisis will be escalated or de-escalated and a child humanized or dehumanized.

It is evident that schoolteachers are fully aware of the impact they have on student learning but may not connect other such actions to the social-emotional growth of students. It is important for all K–12 educators to understand the power and influence they have on the EQ of their students. This is true both inside and outside of the classroom. Thus, if schools are to take seriously the social-emotional wellness of students, all components of the educational program should become a conduit for developing their emotional intelligence (Berkowitz, 2012b).

The Ultimate Goal: Emotional Intimacy

The ultimate questions to be answered in regard to growing emotionally intelligent young people are: For what purpose? What is the end goal? These are valid questions. Is it simply enough to understand oneself and other's emotions? Is the goal simply to produce good citizens? Or is it that we desire something more? As humans, we desire connection with others. And while most connections remain surface level, and that is fine, there are certain individuals with whom we desire a deeper level of connection. There are those in our lives who we feel a deep bond with and want to know better and be more fully known by.

You may recall, for the purposes of this book, intimacy is defined as "to fully know and be fully known, without fear of rejection." For many of us, this is a great challenge. In fact, it may be harder for us to let another know us intimately for fear of rejection than it is to seek to know another more fully. Often, we find that people are more willing to overlook the flaws in others than accept the flaws within. Much of this fear comes as a result of how our emotional intelligence was shaped as we grew. If our developmental experiences as children were such that we learned to suppress our emotions and hide who we were, then we are not readily willing to share those as an adult.

Yet, "being fully known and understood requires that we say aloud to someone else what is going on in our souls" (Yerkovich and Yerkovich, 2017, p. 19). This is the power of growing emotionally intelligent young people; they feel comfortable outwardly expressing what they are experiencing internally. Affording young people these types of experiences during their formative years will have a powerful impact on their ability to develop deep connections as adults.

How we respond to students in a time of emotional distress has a greater impact than we are aware of on how they will respond in similar situations to others as adults. Young people who did not have positive experiences or receive comfort during times of emotional distress do not grow to understand it (Yerkovich and Yerkovich, 2017). As adults, they often mimic their experiences during their growing years. This can make growing emotionally intimate with a significant other very difficult. With the lack of emphasis on emotional intelligence in homes and schools today, as well as society overall, it is no wonder the divorce rate continues to rise. We are not provided the tools for growing emotionally intimate with another.

One thing that has been demonstrated over and over through the years is our need to form bonds with others. Adults with children, who have strong bonds with their parents, recognize this need in their children. More often this is manifested in maternal relationships, though not solely or always. These are the parents who when they see that a child is upset, hurt, or sad comfort the child and use the opportunity to form a stronger bond with them. Parents who did not receive this type of comforting can struggle to see it as a bonding experience with their children.

It is important at this time to clarify the difference between emotional intimacy and emotional dependency. As stated earlier, emotional intimacy is to fully know and be fully known, without fear of rejection, whereas emotional dependency is when a person believes they need another person to be happy or feel complete (www.mindbodygreen.com). Marcus Warner and Chris Coursey (2019), in their book *The 4 Habits of Joy-Filled Marriages*, explain that the brain forms two types of attachments that they entitle *fear bonds* and *joy bonds*. These types of bonds apply to all types of relationships, not just familial ones.

A fear bond is an attachment in which we are never quite sure where we stand with the other person (p. 44). A joy bond is an attachment to someone in which we feel secure (p.44). These two types of bonds are particularly true for students. Fear bonds are prevalent in students who come from abusive homes. This can carry over to the classroom where the students' natural bond with the teacher may be one of fear. Regardless, all students seek a joy bond with an adult figure. For many, that opportunity may only be available to them in the classroom.

Bonding and the Role of the Teacher

One of the most influential variables in human development is social relationships (Berkowitz, 2012b). In addition, research indicates that students long for caring relationships with adults (Chambers et al., 2005). Research from the field of psychology supports these findings. As stated previously, developmental theorists and empirical research have substantiated the importance of fostering positive relationships between young people and adults (Whitted, 2011).

Most people can point to a teacher or group of teachers and talk about the positive or negative role they played in their life. It is not uncommon to hear stories of how a teacher had a positive impact on a person's learning, athletic development, or career interests. However, it is rare to read stories of specifically how a teacher helped a student develop a positive approach to dealing with and expressing emotions.

While the average educator may not be classified as a trendsetter, the fact remains that students often emulate some of their teachers' characteristics and behaviors. Simply due to the amount of exposure teachers have to their students on a day-to-day basis, educators play an important role in shaping the EQ of children. Elkind and Sweet (2004) remind us that as teachers, we play a significant role in the EQ development of a student, whether we believe we are or not. Teachers help shape the character and emotional competence of the students we come in contact with; it's in the way we talk, the behaviors we model, the conduct we tolerate, the deeds we encourage, and the expectations we transmit.

So, what does all this mean? Simply put, the first duty of a teacher in shaping student development is to understand that he or she is a role model. While it is true that students will be exposed to multiple persons in the larger culture who in some manner or another will serve as a role model (star athletes, musicians, actors/actresses, etc.), with the exception of a parent, the teacher is the one person with whom the student will interact in person on a daily basis. As stated previously, the teacher may be the sole person a student develops a joy bond with.

It is true that parents most often have the most impactful role when modeling behaviors for their children. The problem is that a growing number of children do not live in a home where both parents reside. Many of these students are raised by single parents, or in foster homes, or by grandparents. By no means does this suggest this is a recipe for failure. However, the challenges facing adults in these situations put a strain on time and energy to a point that interactions are greatly reduced (especially in cases where the single parent has to work multiple jobs to make ends meet). Thus, the adults' ability to influence the child's emotional intelligence growth in a positive manner is reduced.

The second thing teachers need to consider is how to reframe their thinking about classroom rules. Most students look at classroom rules and regulations from a fear bond perspective. It is not that rules are a bad thing—expectations for classroom behaviors are a positive thing to instill in students. However, educators need to move away from rules and regulations that focus mainly on preventing problem behaviors by following a prescribed list of "dos and don'ts" and toward strategies for teaching normative practices in the classroom. Normative practices are those that focus on teaching positive social skills and foster student growth in emotional intelligence.

The emphasis here is on relationship. Rules in and of themselves, without a positive relationship being built and the chance to practice positive behaviors, will not result in the positive EQ growth of the student. Building relationships with stakeholders (students), combined with the development of routines, will result in positive results for students (Vincent and Grove, 2013). These results incorporate all aspects of a student's life: academic, social, and emotional.

SUMMARY

This chapter seeks to give you a better understanding of what we mean when referring to someone's emotional intelligence and to remind you of the power and importance of relationships. Additionally, it seeks to stress the power and influence teachers have on their students both in and out of the classroom. And probably most importantly, it seeks to emphasize the important role the teacher plays in the development of student emotional intelligence.

Possibly the greatest challenge for teachers is found in the reality that school programs are limited in the amount of time with which they can work with students before they return to a larger society. In a large societal setting, students are confronted with hours of exposure to multiple offerings that can counteract the efforts of even the best teachers. If teachers are to be successful in their efforts of developing students' emotional intelligence, it will require efforts that extend beyond the school day and focus on giving individual students the tools, understanding, and resolve needed to remain positive in an ever-challenging world.

Chapter 3

Self-awareness, Society, and Growing Emotional Intelligence

WHAT'S WRONG WITH ME? WHY SHOULD I CARE?

Have you ever heard a student say, "I don't know what's wrong with me? Why am I angry all the time?" Or, ask it as a question, "what's wrong with me?" because they believed they were wrong to feel anger or sadness? Think about the circumstances under which it happened. How did you respond? The questions that we ask ourselves regarding emotions and feelings, and how we answer them, tell us a lot about our EQ.

Understanding our EQ and helping our students grow emotionally strong starts with an awareness of how we view our own emotions and those of others. It is not uncommon to meet a person who holds the belief that their emotion, or the way they feel, is what is wrong. This is particularly true of younger people. Many believe there is something *wrong* with them when they experience negative emotions more so than others. This is a sign of an immature level of EQ.

A person with a more mature EQ is aware of his or her feelings and knows that the emotion he or she is feeling, in and of itself, is not wrong. Such people are capable of delineating the emotion from the behavior as appropriate or inappropriate. They trust their feelings and learn that it is their actions that might need to be changed, not their emotions. They recognize that feeling sad, angry, or grouchy is just as valid as feeling happy, relaxed, or confident.

Too often in our culture we read about people who have committed some horrific crime only to find out their rage and hatred was the result of suppressed emotions. These are people who never came to understand their emotions due to the lack of opportunity to express them in a healthy manner.

They grow to believe their emotions are wrong and bury them deep inside as a means of regulating them. Their end goal is to be more like the Vulcan race of *Star Trek* fame.

You may or may not be aware of who the Vulcans were. Vulcans were a fictional extraterrestrial humanoid race character on the hit television series, and subsequent movies, *Star Trek* (Wikipedia, Star Trek). They were logical beings void of emotions. The most famous of these people was Mr. Spock. Yet, Spock was half-human and often struggled as a result of trying to remove emotion from his daily life. He struggles to adopt *Surak's* code of emotional control. It is this character that builds a movement upon logical thinking and emotion-repressing (Wikipedia, Surak).

Unintentionally, school discipline structures lead some students to struggle from this same construct. These students believe that logical thinking is what is important and that emotions need to be suppressed. As stated previously, these are the students who believe there is something wrong with them when they experience negative emotions. They have internalized the notion that feeling angry is bad and stunts one's personal growth. As a result, these students often will have the same facial expression whether happy or sad, angry or afraid. This lack of emotional response becomes a challenge to teachers wanting to help students grow emotionally strong.

Consider the following scenario. A student receives a gift from a peer. The student is encouraged to open the gift immediately but is hesitant. Eventually the student acquiesces and opens the gift. He is appreciative but shows little emotion that would let the giver and others know if he is excited or happy about what he has received. The immediate reaction of the giver is one of hurt due to the assumption that he does not like the gift. A simple smile may be all that is expressed. Yet, the reality is that the receiver of the gift was greatly excited, just not sure how to react due to personal experiences and upbringing. This is most likely due to one of three possibilities.

The first is simply a matter that the student may feel uncertain of how to respond or react. Receiving a gift under such circumstances may make the student feel awkward and uncomfortable. The second is somewhat similar. Different students react differently to their emotions (Gladwell, 2005). We talk more about this in detail later in the book. Suffice it to say, for some of us, it is a challenge to understand another's response due to the nature of how we would have responded in that circumstance.

It is the third possibility that requires more attention. These students repress positive emotions as readily as negative ones. Repression of positive emotions can have as negative of an impact as repressing negative ones. Most often, the repression of positive emotions is a learned response. In such cases, students learned over time that outward displays of emotions are inappropriate. In fact, in such cultures, this is the norm. To be clear, this is not to pass judgment on any particular cultural practices. It is simply to point out their impact on student EQ development.

Teachers often overlook that this way of thinking and acting is accentuated in the homes. Expression of emotion is simply not allowed. Yet, we are well aware that, as humans, we have feelings and need to find means for expressing them in a positive manner. For some, particularly those who have not been permitted to express emotions openly, their only opportunities for emotional expression have occurred in solitude. The irony is that many of us do not do well with solitude because of the very emotions we feel. As humans, we are wired to avoid pains associated with our emotions. Solitude accentuates our awareness of these pains.

Solitude and silence can be hard on us emotionally. We desire so much to be understood and open expression of emotions is one means for revealing our true nature. Even so, there are some benefits to the solitude and silence. Those with a stronger EQ see solitude from a positive perspective. These are the ones who view the quietness as an opportunity to allow one's soul to catch up with the rest of the body due to overly busy schedules. These folks, though, tend to be older and have come to see the silence as a time to name the emotions they are feeling. For most students, the reality exists that solitude and silence are a time for uneasiness and angst.

So what are teachers to do? Our education and training has not prepared us for these challenges. Even so, we struggle to find the time to work with students on this level. Time is one of the greatest challenges schools face in educating students, academically and emotionally. This is our reality: school programs are limited in the amount of time with which they can work with students. At the end of each day, students return to the larger society in which hours of exposure to contradicting viewpoints can counteract the efforts of even the best programs. But if we are going to take on the challenge of growing student EQ, we must be willing to start somewhere. So, where?

The best place to start is in your classroom if you are a teacher or in your office if a counselor or administrator. And it does not have to be a matter of arranging the time for it. It starts with a recognition of our own humanity. Simply put, it starts with an awareness of self and an acceptance that we are emotional beings as well. It may seem like a strange dichotomy, but we began the process of looking outward by looking inward. Research reveals that adults who are able to process and understand their own emotions are better able to support young people in processing their own (Gottman, 1997).

The question then is: "What does it mean to be self-aware of our emotions?" We have already established that as humans, we are by nature, emotional beings. But let's make sure to set the record straight, being an emotional being does not imply that we make our feelings apparent at all times. As discussed previously, people express emotions in differing ways. Plenty of people experience feelings internally without expressing them outwardly. Research supports that such people can be emotionally aware without being highly expressive (Gottman, 1997).

According to John Gottman (1997), self-awareness comprised three components: (1) you recognize when you are feeling an emotion; (2) you can specifically identify the emotion and; (3) you are sensitive to the presence of emotions in others (p. 76). There are those that might question component #1. After all, we have established that, as humans, we are emotional beings. Therefore, we recognize when we are feeling an emotion. Observations suggest that there are times where this is not the case.

So, why would this be the case? One example would be a person who is experiencing *dissociation*. Dissociation occurs when a person becomes disconnected from their thoughts, *feelings*, memories, or surroundings (WebMD .com). While dissociation is usually temporary, it is a source of disconnect for recognizing when we are experiencing an emotion. While some psychologists consider dissociation as abnormal, Sigmund Freud regarded it as a normal means of self-defense of the mind (Davies, 2010).

Regarding component #2, there are a variety of reasons a person may not be able to identify an emotion they are experiencing. Sometimes the reason may be as simple as the person is experiencing mixed emotions and is unable to process the different feelings. This is most often seen in people who have experienced a fearful situation and the fear merges with anger as the event plays out. It may even be that the person is experiencing an emotion they have never experienced previously. This is more likely to occur in younger children, yet is still a possibility. I recall the time I suddenly felt a strange sense of nervousness I had never felt before. It was later explained that it was a feeling of anxiety.

One of the greatest challenges we may face in identifying an emotion is that we do not know the term for it. For example, one emotion that began to expose itself during the COVID-19 pandemic could be identified as "Acedia." *Acedia* is a Greek term referring to a lack of care or concern for one's surroundings or the condition of the world. And while the term is most often referred to as *apathy* in the English language, or associated with depression, it remains an emotion many of us cannot identify.

Still, the matter remains, as teachers, if we are to be sensitive to the emotions of our students, we must begin with an awareness of our own. And while there may be times we struggle with being self-aware, we recognize that self-awareness of one's emotions is a reflection of one's personal EQ. To that extent, growing emotionally intelligent students requires we focus on our own EQ growth as well. And the importance of emotional self-awareness cannot be overstated.

The Importance of Self-awareness

The first thing to understand is that, as teachers, we come to a classroom as a person with more than just the perspective of an educator. We are family members, friends, and colleagues as well. A lot of what we have come to understand about young people and their behavior comes from experiences we have encountered through our life's journey in these varying roles. The fact is that teachers find themselves on many journeys in their lifetime, some simultaneous (e.g., the journey of parenthood concurrent with the journey of classroom teaching). Yes, life as a teacher is a journey. Along this journey we come to understand who we are, who our students are, and how we make a difference.

Have you ever asked yourself any of the following questions? Am I aware of my emotions when working with others? How do I show emotions to others? Do I mask them? Do I manage them? Do I thrive when others need me? Do I have a need to be needed by others? How you answer these questions reflects your level of EQ.

One of the first, and maybe most important indicators, of our personal EQ is our ability to be aware of our own feelings. According to Daniel Goleman (1995), "Self-awareness—recognizing a feeling as it happens—is the keystone of emotional intelligence" (p. 43). Awareness of our own feelings directly affects how well we tune into the feelings of others. This awareness serves as a compass and plays a role in helping others grow in EQ. As a teacher, you must remember that others learn by watching and by allowing others to see that we have feelings, we allow them to feel more confident about their own feelings.

Of course, this can only happen in a positive manner when we are aware of our emotions and respond to them appropriately. This can be challenging at times. Emotions are as numerous and as diverse as trees in a forest. And understanding which emotion we may be feeling at any one moment could be as difficult as choosing a particular treat in a candy store. We often vacillate between a number of choices.

We must also understand that emotions manifest themselves in many ways. Two people may not respond the same way to a specific emotion. For example, people who are angry may not manifest that anger with the same behavior—one may choose to punch something while another represses it within, and yet another goes to the gym to work off his aggression. The important thing is that we are able to clue into the various behaviors that we, and others, exhibit and understand that the behavior often indicates a specific emotion.

As such, an important part of the EQ growth process is developing an awareness of our own emotions and understanding that having such feelings is OK. Being EQ mature is reflected by how comfortable we are with sharing our feelings and allowing others to do so as well. We should feel free to express disappointment, show sadness, and even express feelings of anger or fear and feel comfortable with others doing so as well. As a teacher, this is important because it helps others better understand that everyone feels emotions and that the way we feel is usually not the problem.

Many years of observation suggest that most teachers are aware of their students' emotions when they *act out*. However, on most occasions, observations revealed that the teacher was less aware of his own emotions at the time. As we will see, awareness of one's own emotions is an important characteristic. In fact, it is an essential component of addressing student displays of emotion. A teacher's awareness of her own feelings has a direct impact on how she responds to the student and tunes into the student's emotional needs (Gottman, 1997).

Let's not lose sight of the fact that good teaching involves emotion! Emotions not only are a part of every aspect of our lives, but they also play an important role. Awareness of our emotions is paramount to our success. Research demonstrates that your emotional awareness and ability to manage feelings, more than IQ, determine your success in relationships and all walks of life (Gottman, 1997). And, it is important that we remember that students learn by watching. As such, demonstrating awareness of one's own emotions and responding appropriately has a positive impact on student EQ growth.

Thus, an important component in the process of growing emotionally intelligent students is the willingness of teachers to allow their students to see that they also have feelings. This helps students come to a better understanding that we are all emotional beings. More importantly, allowing students to see that we have feelings exemplifies what we hope they will understand that feeling a particular way is not wrong or problematic. This is why teachers should feel free to express disappointment, show sadness, and even express feelings of anger or fear.

This is not to suggest teachers demonstrate fear of their students. Rather, the "fear" referred to here is a healthy type of fear, such as when a teacher makes a student aware that they were afraid he or she may have been hurt by their actions. In doing so, students understand that the teacher genuinely cares for them. Sharing this type of fear creates openness, aids in the trust-building process, and can serve as an effective demonstration of expressing emotions. And students need to come to an understanding that it is OK to have fears.

This is particularly true for students of this generation as the list of fear types is continually growing. For example, *nomophobia*, the fear of being detached from our cell phones, is a reality for students today. Regardless of our personal thoughts on this issue, we must be careful not to dismiss the fear (we will talk more in detail about the dangers of dismissal later), rather focus on helping students' growth in emotional intelligence in order to not be held captive by it. Again, being open and honest about our own fears helps students develop a sense of acceptance of theirs.

With that said, it is important for educators to remember that showing personal emotion does not mean that students can meet your emotional needs. Teacher expression of emotion is not for the purpose of getting the students to like you. The goal is to grow students' emotion quotients. Research reflects that students have better academic results and are more cooperative with teachers who support them in a positive manner (Chambers et al., 2005) and trust them (Gregory and Ripski, 2008).

With all that as a backdrop, we now must return to where we started and ask ourselves the following questions:

Am I aware of my emotions when working with my students?
How do I show emotions to my students—do I mask them or do I manage them?
Do I thrive when students need me?
Or, do I have a need to be needed by my students?

By honestly answering these questions, teachers get a better understanding of how a personal display of emotion impacts student display of emotion. The key is to keep in mind that the goal is to model for students on how to balance emotions and behaviors. It is not on meeting the teacher's emotional needs. While teacher's personal wellness is important and needs to be cultivated, what we focus on here is student growth in emotional intelligence.

Culture and Definitions: Their Impact on EQ

One of the hidden barriers to our work with growing emotionally intelligent students comes in a form we do not often consider, how we personally define the terms we use and our understanding of them. As teachers, we often develop classroom expectations that include very important dispositions, behaviors, and actions students should demonstrate. For example, we often see a posting in elementary school settings, with something about the expectation of acting *responsibly*. No one would argue that *being responsible* is important. However, as teachers, we must remember to take into account that since being responsible is an action verb, it is best defined by the specific behaviors to be exhibited.

While most people have a general understanding of what *responsibility* looks like in action, to a student there may be some misconceptions. During their formative years, a young student's understanding of responsibility will most often come from the home. But, in some homes, being responsible has not been modeled well, and the student fails to fully understand what the teacher's expectations are. The student may think they are demonstrating responsibility through a certain action when their actions may not be appropriate. As teachers, we need to ensure our thoughts and notions on such behaviors are made clear to the students.

An example of the need to develop a common definition of key terms for students is the following:

A high school student understands the importance of attending classes on time and regularly. He comes everyday prepared for class with all necessary supplies. He completes all homework assignments on time and in detail. He is well organized and uses his time well. Yet he does not see it as his responsibility to take good care of school property. He often leaves his work area a mess. When confronted about this by the teacher, he responds that it is the janitor's responsibility to clean up. Further investigation into the life of the student reveals that he is used to others cleaning up after him. He does not see cleaning up after oneself in terms of a responsible behavior.

Before judging the previous example, remember its purpose, to serve as a reminder that students bring different experiences and interpretations to the classroom. Hence, it is important for the teacher, as best as possible, to work with students to build a common definition of terms used when establishing classroom expectations. Equally important is the need to include language in terms of actionable behaviors.

Perhaps a better example of how we define terms and the impact it has on our behavior comes from looking at the term *respect*. Most of us think of *respect* in terms of how it applies as a noun. However, when we refer to it in terms of a verb, in our minds, we associate specific actions with it, forgetting that not everyone sees the term through the same behaviors. Some cultures look at respect as something to be earned while others look at it as something given. Hence, one may see someone's actions as *disrespectful* that someone else sees as a means of earning respect. In such a case, two people could have entirely different emotional responses to the same event. When we are unable to reconcile such differences in understanding, our EQ suffers.

Consider the following example: a high school teacher has a student in his geometry course who has moved here from Korea and is raised in the strictest traditions of that culture. The teacher notices the student will not look him in the eye when talking with him one on one. He feels disrespected and brings this to the father's attention the next time they meet. The father responds by saying that the student better not look him in the eye as it is a sign of disrespect in his culture. The obvious thought here is that the teacher needs to have an understanding of cultural differences. However, consider the challenges for the student.

While it is certainly important for the young man to remain true to familial cultural expectations, a conflict arises in that local cultural expectations may be at odds with some. There are times he will find himself in a setting where he is expected to look the other person in the eye. Consider the impact on the student's emotions as he processes through this dichotomy. The solution may not be as easy as we are led to believe.

The challenge is finding a means of coming to a common understanding. Most would agree that it is important in the places we live and work to act respectfully. But how can this be accomplished if we have differing views? It is an important question to ask and to be answered. The problem is that the answer is not a simple one due to the impact on the community members who don't share a common perspective. Hence, the real challenge teachers face, and must solve, comes in defining words like *respect* in terms of behaviors beyond the local setting and community. If we do not define terms like *respect* from a common perspective, community members feel and react differently to a member's actions. In such cases, our emotions suffer as we struggle to understand the other's actions and feelings.

One possible way to combat this challenge is to take time at the beginning of the school year, or term, to process with students what such terms as respect and responsibility look like in actions. The teacher could start by simply asking students to list five actions they associate with the term respect. After students have made their list individually, they can be paired up with another to share and compare lists. Afterward, the groups of two can be made into groups of four and lists continually compared and constructed. The final step would be to have the small groups compile their lists on chart paper and tape them to a wall. The activity culminates with having students review all charts and mark their top three or four *respect* actions. A list of the top five to ten actions can be compiled, discussed, and agreed upon by all in the class.

As we can see, a great challenge teachers face is that student populations are becoming more heterogeneous. In many cases, there are fewer family supports in the homes. While the impact of fewer family supports on student behavior is readily accepted, one could easily question what bearing having more heterogeneous groupings would have on student behavior in the classroom. This matter can best be understood by considering the role culture plays upon student actions as demonstrated previously.

As discussed in chapter 1, a good representation of this construct within education is found in Dr. Ruby Payne's work *A Framework for Understanding Poverty: A Cognitive Approach*. In her research, Dr. Payne (1995) discovered that the "hidden values" students of differing socioeconomic levels bring to the classroom impact their understanding of specific constructs (e.g., respect and responsibility) and thus their behaviors. The adult's response to such behaviors, be it empathetic or punitive, plays an indirect role in how the student processes the event internally, consequently impacting emotional growth and intelligence.

Hence, hidden deep within school and classroom expectations is the need to construct more affective systems for developing student cultural understanding and emotional intelligence. In doing so, teachers indirectly teach expectations that allow for increased time spent on academics rather than responding to disruptive behaviors (Hansen, 2014). Even more importantly, the impact of doing so is significant in the development of student emotional intelligence.

SUMMARY

In order to help students grow in emotional intelligence, we must begin with an understanding of how we process our own emotions and view those of others. It is not uncommon to meet a person who holds the belief that the emotion, or way they feel, is what is wrong with them. A person with a strong EQ is aware of their feelings and is accepting of their emotions. They recognize it is not wrong to feel certain ways. They are capable of deciphering the emotion from the behavior as appropriate or inappropriate. They trust their feelings and recognize that feeling sad, angry, or grouchy is just as valid as feeling happy, relaxed, or confident.

People with a strong emotional intelligence recognize that differing emotions may reflect conflicting perspectives or understanding of a particular matter or construct. As such, teachers must acknowledge this conflict and work to ensure that everyone has a common understanding in such matters. By doing so, the teacher is growing not only individual emotional intelligence but group EQ as well. According to research, group EQ is high when a team trusts each other, as a sense of oneness or identity, and can work together to produce positive results. Finding a common identity often requires looking for commonalities where we traditionally do not. This is important in a society that is becoming more heterogeneous and culturally diverse.

More and more, young people are developing their understanding of societal expectations through social networking, popular culture, and mass media. This is having a profound impact on their emotional intelligence growth and subsequently, emotional wellness. Further compounding the problem is the fact that over the past century, the economy of the United States has shifted from a focus on mass production to one of mass consumption. This, too, has had a profound impact on the psychological and emotional well-being of students as the ethical requirements placed on students has begun to shift as well. According to the Character Education Partnership (2005), with growing abundance, more emphasis is being placed upon accumulation and the cultivation of personal preferences than on a sense of community and emotional wellness.

As such, the need for schools to become a conduit for growth in student emotional intelligence, as well as cultural awareness, grows bigger by the year. Schools that serve as caring communities go beyond the core academic content and consider the social and emotional well-being of their students to be a priority (Berkowitz, 2012b; Doyle and Doyle, 2003). A caring school community is one that "has an *ethic of care* that works to develop students who will become empathetic adults and transport a caring mission beyond the walls of the school into their communities" (Doyle and Doyle, 2003, p. 259). Caring schools recognize the varying developmental needs of students and cultivate emotional intelligence as part of the growth process.

Chapter 4

Teaching and Cultivating
Emotional Intelligence

TEACHING AND COMING TO
A FRIGHTENING CONCLUSION

Many educators across the nation talk about the need to infuse efforts aimed at growing student emotional intelligence into their school program. Rightfully so, it is a key element missing from the work schools are doing with their student body in terms of social and emotional development. As teachers, we share a common understanding that a quality social-emotional learning effort will have a positive impact on a school's climate and culture. Still, when teachers and administrators gather around to discuss the idea of implementing a formal program, one faculty member inevitably asks: Why do we need to teach this stuff? The implication of the question is: Should it not be taught in the home?

As discussed previously, most teachers agree with the important role parents play in the moral, social and emotional development of their child(ren). However, the reality is that many students across the nation come from broken homes, or ones where parents do not specifically address or model the topic in the home. As such, if schools and families do not address emotional intelligence and the resulting impact on social behaviors, it is likely that students will learn social behaviors through means that may not always be positive (e.g., social media and negative role models) will increase dramatically.

Teachers often point out how students look to them for support, encouragement, and direction because it is lacking at home, probably more often than they care to admit. The impact a teacher can have on the mood and emotion, and subsequently the EQ development, of a student is immense. One often-used quote in understanding this notion comes from Haim Ginott (first introduced in chapter 2), an Israeli teacher, child psychologist, psychotherapist, and a parent educator. I can think of no better quote to offer at this time as to the power of reflection and the importance of understanding one's actions and resulting impact on the development of student emotional intelligence.

The quote comes from his book *Teacher and Child: A Book for Parents and Teacher*:

> I've come to the frightening conclusion that I am the decisive element in the classroom. My personal approach creates the climate. My daily mood makes the weather. As a teacher, I possess a tremendous power to make a child's life miserable or joyous. I can be a tool of torture or an instrument of inspiration. I can humiliate or humor, hurt or heal. In all situations, it is my response that decides whether a crisis will be escalated or de-escalated and a child humanized or dehumanized.

Only recently has the development of student EQ been seen as an integral part of education. Yet, think back to the various adults who served in a teaching capacity during your formative years and try to recall how their mood set the climate in the room and how they made you feel by their words and actions. Did they build you up or cut you down? Were they easily forgotten or did they have a lasting impact? These are the things that played an important role in your EQ development. Now consider how you respond to your students and others as a teacher. Do you humiliate or instill confidence? Do you hurt or heal?

Our words and actions as teachers and building administrators are often overlooked in terms of the role they play in the cultivation and growth of the EQ of individuals under our care. Teachers with strong personal EQs know how to respond during challenging moments in a manner that de-escalates the situation, rather than escalates it into a crisis. They recognize the impact their response to students has. They seek to humanize rather than dehumanize. They work to build others up rather than cut them down. How you see yourself in these circumstances reflects your own personal EQ growth and development.

As teachers, we need to consider not only the words we choose to use, but the ways in which we speak them. It is more often the way in which we say something that incites conflict or adverse reactions from students, than the words themselves. While content matters (what we mean to say), so does attitude or how we say it. How we say something can often leave a student feeling as disrespected as what we say. Just because a student does not act out does not mean he or she does not feel disrespected. Many students choose to shut down in such circumstances. Consider the long-term impact of the manner in which we speak on the student's emotional intelligence development.

Students who shut down in response to negative emotions as a coping mechanism present a unique challenge to teachers. Sometimes a word or action by the teacher creates a response from a student that comes from something far deeper than the topic at hand. This makes it difficult for the teacher to decipher what is truly going on inside the student. We don't get a glimpse of the true picture. What seems to be the issue is not the issue at all. These are the times where teachers must learn to read a student's countenance, or read into their words, as they may often reflect a more serious issue than we understand. It is imperative for teachers to engage the student and empathize with them (we will discuss empathy in more detail later in the book).

When we, as teachers, take the time to engage students who are feeling angry, frustrated, or hurt, we find that there is an issue the student is struggling with that is deeper than the apparent issue at hand. By engaging students in dialogue that brings such matters to the surface, the teacher helps humanize the student and defuse negative emotions that may be on the verge of spiraling out of control. Sometimes the easiest means for defusing conflict is taking the time to discern what is truly going on inside the student.

Think back to earlier when we discussed the idea of emotional intimacy, the idea that as humans, we desire to know and be fully known without fear of rejection (Wagner and McGee, 2016). If we truly desire to help students grow in emotional intelligence, then a first step to take is letting them know we desire to fully know them and that it is OK for them to be fully known. While we cannot promise others may not reject them, we can confirm and make it clear that we will not. In doing so, we model for our students what it means to be accepting of another, an important step in growing emotional intelligence. Still, modeling remains a great challenge for teachers.

More often than not, it is far easier for a teacher to get to know their students than it is to allow them to fully know them. One reason is many of us have not seen this practice modeled and are uncertain of, or have little practice as to, actions for doing so. Let's be honest, opening ourselves up to being fully known by our students is difficult because of the fear it may expose deficiencies in who we are. As teachers, we must give the appearance that we have our lives all together when deep down inside, we know this is not always the truth. This means that even as teachers, we must be willing to surrender some of the things about ourselves we prefer to keep hidden. Maybe it is a divorce in our past, or an embarrassment suffered as a child. Things we consider a black mark on our being that would actually serve to humanize us in our students' eyes.

The truth is that there are moments in all our lives that we want to keep hidden or that we are not proud of, but they do not define who we are. They are snapshots of a time gone by. This is equally true of our students. And while the snapshots may be true, they do not define who our students are either.

Consider though, that just as we found passage into a new way of life even though wounded, so too can we be a source of inspiration for our students to do so. Our stories may be the one element students need to know to remove the anger, bitterness, or depression that keeps them from bringing the buried grief they house to the surface as they seek a passage into a new way of life as well.

It is easy to draw false conclusions about someone based upon one small lapse in judgment or poor decision. As such, it makes sense that teachers and students both choose to hide these times. However, if, as teachers, our desire is to grow emotionally intelligent students, the importance of exposing such times may be more important than we care to accept. Remember, when students come to understand that they are not alone in letting emotions get the better of them, they begin the emotional intelligence growth process. It is equally true for teachers as well.

Probably the most important aspect of this reasoning is that growth in emotional intelligence occurs relationally. Students do not grow in emotional intelligence by being told or taught how they should feel and react. They grow through experience, dialogue, and modeling. As teachers, we must understand that just as our experiences shaped our emotional growth, so will our students' personal experiences. Dialogue about such experiences is a key component of the emotional intelligence development of students.

Dialogue between teachers and students can be difficult when it comes to emotional experiences. The key is to remember that dialogue is used to help us develop a sense of self-awareness and awareness of others. According to Jim Knight (2015), dialogue helps us understand who we are in relation to others and the world in which we live. This understanding is a vital part of a strong EQ. Thus, in essence, it becomes a moral imperative for teachers to model and provide for dialogic engagement both inside and outside the classroom walls.

In the end, maybe the frightening conclusion we must come to as teachers is the reality that we are not much different than our students. We have simply had more opportunities for growth through our experiences. We understand the value of dialogue with peers and friends in walking our journey. Our challenge is to answer the question on how we provide those same opportunities for our students in an effort to help them grow emotionally strong.

Thus, the questions to be answered remain: Have you come to any frightening conclusions about yourself? Do you see yourself as the decisive element in the classroom in creating a positive climate? As a teacher, do you recognize the tremendous power you possess to make a child's life miserable or joyous? Are you a tool of torture or an instrument of inspiration? Do you humiliate or humor, hurt or heal? Most importantly, how do you view the impact of such actions, words, and behaviors on the social-emotional learning of your students?

It's Not Fair! The Importance of How We Define Fairness

Not long ago my oldest daughter gave me a blank journal entitled *A Father's Story*. Each page of the book is blank with one exception, the question at the top. The purpose is for my daughter to get to know me and my story more deeply. One question caught my eye right away: *Do you think life's fair?* The very first sentence I wrote simply stated: "The answer to this question lies in your definition of 'fair.'" If we think of fairness as everyone getting the same thing under the same circumstances, or that life is balanced for everyone equally, then the answer is obviously "no." One only needs to look at the outside world to see life is not fair under these terms.

Before we go any further with this, let's be clear there is a difference between "unfair" and "unjust." Here we are focusing on the construct of "fairness." If, by contrast to the previous definition of "fair," we mean that each person is provided the same opportunity for growth and happiness, even if it is a harder journey for some, then we are like-minded. To see from this perspective, one must accept that bad things do happen to good people.

Why does this matter? It matters simply because the way you view *fairness* in life has a direct impact on your personal EQ development. Those who see life as unfair because some have more than others often struggle with manifesting their emotions in a positive way. People whose EQ development is more mature may at times ask "what if?" but rarely, if ever, ask "why me?" And while there is a time and place for the application of each definition, one must strive to not let negative emotions display themselves through inappropriate behaviors when one believes something is "unfair." Being able to respond in a positive manner during such times reveals a person with a strong EQ.

Have you ever watched the movie *The Lion King*? The focus of the movie can be narrowed to two characters desiring the same goal, to one day become king. If you have seen the movie, you know that Simba, the reigning king's son, is next in line to be king simply due to being the first-born son. His uncle, Scar, the king's younger brother had been next in line prior to the birth of his nephew. A key scene in the movie occurs as Scar captures a mouse for lunch and takes the time to explain to it that life is simply not fair. He equates the mouse's situation to his losing the throne to his nephew simply by birthright. One could accept from the mouse's perspective how life was not fair, but question Scar's reason for self-pity.

What do Scar and Simba and their self-pity have to do with emotional intelligence you may ask? If you have seen the movie, then you will recognize how the emotions of these two characters are manifested throughout, all as a result of how they define "fair." Simba is a child at the beginning of the movie and we get a chance to observe his emotional growth, all as a result of the adults (teachers) who take an active role in his life. We see him become a confident king.

By contrast, Scar, being older and more set in his ways, displays the negative emotions he is experiencing, mainly anger, in more deceitful and harmful manners. He does not hesitate to bully or manipulate. Even his cowardice is a pretense for the ignoble acts he cunningly devises. It may seem like a stretch to tie it back to his statement on life and fairness, but it certainly is a manifestation of the level of his emotional intelligence, his EQ.

This is not to suggest that one stops growing in emotional intelligence at some point in one's life. Or to suggest that a person with a low EQ is going to act in deceitful and immoral ways. However, it does suggest that our viewpoint of what is fair and unfair, and even just and unjust, in life, does have an impact on our emotional intelligence development and our impact on our students' growth as well.

In education, the concept of fairness is often associated with consistency of actions, consequences, and materials. What is done for, or to, one person, must happen for all. This notion is often referred to as *rigid equality*. As a construct, *rigid equality* finds its origins in Orwell's work titled *Animal House*. In chapter 9, Wells writes how "a too rigid equality in rations . . . would have been contrary to principles of Animalism" (1945). The themes of the book are focused around equality and inequality, power and control (https://www.bbc.co.uk). As a practice, *rigid equality* has been in place for centuries.

Those who oppose the application of rigid equality as a practice often refer to a picture of three males, wanting to watch a baseball match from outside the wooden outfield fence. Only one of the boys is tall enough to see over the fence, the others are too short. In the picture, each boy has been given a box to stand on to help overcome this issue, but the shortest of the boys is still unable to see over the fence. The idea being that fairness defined as rigid equality, all three boys given exactly the same experience, failed to fully benefit all. This picture is usually followed by one entitled *equity*. In the equity photo, the boy who does not need his box gives it to the shortest boy who, with it, can now see over the fence. The idea being that although one boy received more than another, they all had the same benefit.

In the original picture, the shortest boy could easily have declared "life is not fair," even though given the same exact benefit as others. Emotionally, he would struggle to understand how this idea of fairness helped him at all. Without an opportunity to express his emotions in a healthy manner and proper adult interaction, his emotional intelligence development would be stunted. In other words, this application of fairness could potentially be toxic to this young man.

One of the problems is that the pictures do not portray an accurate picture of what educators face. The notion presented in both pictures is that one boy lacks simply because of the issue of age or heredity (being short). This is presented by showing all three boys standing on level ground, implying that they are all starting from the same vantage point, with the smallest boy's difference in stature being the issue to overcome. One could apply the boy's height to other human dimensions such as a learning ability but that would still not demonstrate the true inequity.

The reality for educators is that students come to them not all starting from the same vantage point. The challenge they face is more realistically portrayed by a picture with three boys of the same height, standing on ground that is sloping downward while the fence slopes upward. The boy standing on the highest ground is starting at a great advantage. He needs little supports. The boy at the lowest vantage point, with the furthest to go, needs far more supports just to get level with the first boy.

In his book *You Can't Teach through a Rat: And Other Epiphanies for Educators*, Dr. Marvin Berkowitz (2012a) refers to three types of children teachers find in the classrooms; he refers to them as the *Golden*, the *Invulnerable*, and the *Tarnished* child. The boy standing on one box on high ground would be an example of a *Golden* child. He starts from a high vantage point and needs little added support from the teacher. He sees life as more than fair. He has all the love and support he needs at home and probably lacks little that he needs to succeed in life. In fact, he may need little support from his teacher in terms of both his academic and emotional intelligence development.

The second boy in the new picture is standing on slightly lower ground at a point in the fence that is slightly higher than the first boy's vantage point. He needs two boxes in order to see over the fence and watch the game. This is the child Dr. Berkowitz refers to as the *Invulnerable* child. They come to school starting at a disadvantage compared to the *Golden* child, with a little higher barrier in front of them, but has some added adult supports already in place and is determined to beat the odds.

While needing what appears to be only a little more support than the *Golden* child, this student does have a greater need for their teacher in order not to fail at life's major challenges and grow emotionally intelligent. This student often comes from a dysfunctional home, with parents who model all the things you don't want children observing. They have an understanding that life is not fair but are determined to balance the playing field and rely heavily on their teacher to help them balance the inequities.

The third boy in the picture would be standing on the lowest part of the downward sloping ground at a point where the fence is at its highest. These are the students who are "at-risk" and start at a great disadvantage compared to their peers. Dr. Berkowitz refers to them as the *Tarnished* child. These are the students, who desperately need their teachers if they are going to succeed. They not only see life as unfair but are also beaten down by the mantra. They greatly rely on the teacher not only for academic learning but also for growth in emotional intelligence. These students most often come from broken homes and are most often from the lower socioeconomic bracket where parents work two jobs and rarely get time to interact with them while awake.

At this point, you may very well be thinking to yourself, "This is irrelevant, I treat all of my students the same." That is well and good, and it should be noted that this is not suggesting you love anyone of them less than the others. It is good to "treat" students equitably. However, teachers must recognize that some students need more support, patience, and care if they are to overcome the greater barriers they face. As Dr. Berkowitz points out:

> For a Tarnished child, a teacher's love and interest in them can make all the difference in the world. These children have not known such a relationship and typically don't believe they can ever be the object of an adult's unqualified and healthy love. They base their expectancies and interpretations on what they have already experienced. (p. 28)

Consider such expectations on the EQ of such students.

Rigid Equality or Restorative Justice Practices

While the walls surrounding the practice of *rigid equality* in terms of materials and supports for student learning in the classroom have begun to erode, its application in other components of schooling has not. An example of this is the application of codes of conduct. You know the book. The one where rules and consequences for breaking such rules are carved in stone like the Ten Commandments. Regardless of why the offense was committed, the consequence must be applied consistently as a means of being "fair." While many codes of conduct have varying consequence levels for a code broken, the focus remains the same, punishment as a form of correction.

Case in point: one of the underlying problems with schools defining fairness as consistency of practice and consequence is that the punishment for problem behaviors remains the same for any individual who displays a particular inappropriate action regardless of circumstance. If two people fight, they should get the same consequence, period, no matter what the precipitating circumstances. Hidden within this understanding are three underlying assumptions: (1) consistency of consequence is what matters most, not restorative practices; and (2) the root of the problem can be addressed via surface level interventions (e.g., out of school suspension for someone caught smoking in the bathroom); (3) a corollary to #2, that student problem behaviors occur void of any emotion, as discussed previously in chapter 3.

The latter may be argued as effective in terms of curtailing the number of students smoking while at school, especially when considering the limited time and resources schools have available to them to address the topic. However, it ceases to have any meaningful impact on getting students to quit smoking, which should be the ultimate goal. More so, it fails to investigate why the student has taken to smoking and the need to continue to do so beyond the habit-forming properties (e.g., students have shared that it helps them relax). Regarding the first assumption, it needs to be considered with scrutiny.

The assumption that consistency of consequence is what matters most presumes people are more concerned with fairness than the resultant impact of the consequence. While there may be some truth in this for some, others may see little value in it. The reason they see it as unfair is due to their perspective on the role of precipitating events. For them, the events and subsequent feelings justify their behavior. This is something many disciplinary actions do not take into consideration and, as such, fail to address the inappropriate behavior in a redemptive manner.

The resulting impact on social behaviors, and emotional growth, is negligible for these students, if not harmful. While common practice for determining a consequence for problem behaviors is based upon a code of conduct book, the lack of positive impact on the problem behavior remains the same. One could question, what does this have to do with emotional intelligence? The answer is simple; we must not lose sight of the goal of growing emotionally intelligent students. The purpose of the EQ development of students is to have students strengthen self-management and relational skills. Students with strong EQs demonstrate positive social skills.

With that having been said, there is an obligation to discuss other options if the practices of *rigid equality* are in question. One option is to look at consequences from a *contextual justice* perspective. For purposes here, the notion of *contextual justice* refers to consequences applied to a particular behavior as a result of circumstances surrounding the event for the purpose of supplanting a problem behavior, not suppressing it. In other words, the goal of the consequence is to teach positive social skills and help the student's social-emotional growth. Such a process requires dialogue focused not only on the external behavior of the student but the emotions or feelings they were experiencing at the time.

The term "dialogue" has been specifically chosen here for a key purpose. As discussed previously, dialogue helps us understand who we are in relation to others and the world in which we live. According to Jim Knight (2015), dialogue achieves this goal by affording one the opportunity to convey their perspective while seeking to understand the other's. Knight states that the purpose of dialogue is to clarify, provide context and identify false assumptions while listening with empathy, responding in humility, being open to new ideas and suspending assumptions.

With that in mind, let's refer back to the example offered previously of a student given suspension for smoking on campus. In that case, no effort was given to understand the student's reasoning for doing so or to truly find a means of helping the student process the matter and even potentially quit the habit. Supporting this claim is the expansive use of suspension as a consequence of a large variety of problem behaviors. In essence, smoking in the bathroom is akin to fighting, which is akin to derogatory language toward a teacher. By contrast, *contextual justice* first seeks to listen and understand, then apply an appropriate consequence aimed at curtailing the problem behavior. In the case of smoking, a student may be assigned to a smoking cessation class. Similarly, students who fight may be required to attend anger management sessions with a professional or go through coaching to stop bullying behaviors.

Consider the following case scenario: a young lady is caught smoking in the girl's bathroom. The school's policy requires removal from the program for such an offense. However, through dialogue with the student, it is discovered the student went to the bathroom to smoke because she was in distress because of a memory. This day was the one-year anniversary of the death of her baby in utero. The baby had been delivered stillborn. Strict adherence to the code of conduct would require that the student be removed, a consequence some considered "fair" as it had been applied to others. It was clear though that such a consequence would do little to help the student's emotional state. Any consequence needs to help the student work through such a trauma and focus on helping the student grow emotionally strong.

A second option proposed for addressing student problem behaviors in place of a *rigid equality* approach is referred to as a *restorative justice* practices approach. *Restorative practices* are not limited in scope and are more specific to conflict and behaviors committed against others. For example, it is not necessary to use such practices for students who are perpetually late to class or school. *Restorative practices* focus attention on creating conditions for any harm to be repaired, mainly for the purpose of repairing relationships, which have been impacted as a result of the problem behavior.

Such practices begin with consequences that are determined by the community in which the infraction occurs. These consequences may differ from event to event, student to student, but the goal remains the same, helping students learn pro-social behaviors, or overcome an addiction (e.g., bullying), for the purpose of restoring relationships and building community. Such practices usually do not place any financial burden on a school but do require more time than traditional methods of determining consequences and a more concerted effort.

According to Restorative Justice Colorado, the goal of *restorative justice practices* is not punishment of the perpetrator, or even reconciliation, although this can be a side effect, it is to address the needs of the victim, the community, and the offender in learning pro-social behaviors (www.rjcolorado.org). A key part of the process is understanding emotions and growth in that arena. Thus, the focus here is on the impact on how we address student actions and behaviors and the resultant effect on the emotional intelligence development of the individual and on the greater society as a whole.

SUMMARY

The words and actions of educators are often overlooked in terms of the role they play in cultivating and growing the EQ of students. Teachers with strong personal EQs know how to respond during challenging moments in a manner that de-escalates the situation, rather than escalates it. They recognize the impact their responses to students have and that they can set the climate in their classroom and school. They seek to humanize rather than dehumanize.

The way we come to see *fairness* in life has a direct impact on our personal EQ development and that of the students we teach. Those who see life as unfair because some have more than others often struggle with manifesting their emotions in a positive way. People whose EQ development is more mature may at times ask "what if?" but rarely, if ever, ask "why me?" As such, one must strive to display negative emotions in appropriate ways, even when one believes they have been treated "unfairly." Being able to respond in a positive manner during such times reveals a person with a strong EQ.

Finally, the practice of *rigid equality* begs two questions: "Does rigid equality in the application of consequences truly imply fairness?" and "What is the impact of such an approach on student growth in positive social skills and emotional intelligence?" The resulting impact of rigid consequences on social behaviors and emotional growth is negligible. Educators must seek other options for addressing problem student behaviors if they truly desire to teach positive social skills to their students and assist them in growing emotionally intelligent.

Chapter 5

Reframing Our Perspectives

INTRODUCTION

In her book *Reflections for Tending the Sacred Garden: Embracing the Art of Slowing Down*, Bonita Zimmer, citing Robert Fulgham, put it simply, "Don't worry that children never listen to you; worry that they are always watching you." One of the greatest impacts a teacher can have on student pro-social behaviors and emotional growth is in the manner in which they respond to displays of emotions. In fact, one of the best ways to gauge one's own EQ level of development is to reflect upon the way one responds to displays of emotion. A true measurement of EQ strength requires that any self-evaluation and introspection be conducted as honestly and uprightly as possible.

The goal of this chapter is to dive a little deeper into cultivating strong student EQ. To help in this effort, we begin by looking at common ways teachers respond to the behaviors of others in light of emotions. Specifically, this chapter introduces four specific approaches to dealing with the emotional behaviors of students. These approaches are referred to throughout as "responses" since they touch on the means by which we respond as educators to student display of emotion. Accordingly, the first three responses discussed are those that have a negative impact on cultivating student EQ. These three are identified using terms that mirror identifiers introduced by Dr. John Gottman in his book *The Heart of Parenting: Raising an Emotionally Intelligent Child*. The three terms are (1) the *dismissive* response, (2) the *disapproving* response, and (3) the *laissez-faire* response.

It should be noted at this time that these categories are generalized and broad in scope. As such, they are not intended to classify adults or teachers in terms of reactionary style or pigeonhole them into one category or another, rather they are simply meant to give an overview of the most common reactions to student display of emotion. In addition, this chapter is not meant to be a treatise on consequences applied to poor choices of behavior, only an investigation as to rationale or reasoning and how such behaviors are addressed.

The Dismissive Response

According to Gottman (1997), the *dismissive* response is one in which the adult treats a young person's expression of emotion as trivial or unimportant. During such times, the adult often feels uncomfortable and annoyed, or even overwhelmed, by these expressions of emotions. Under this umbrella, teachers may believe that the student has little to be sad about or that anger is okay as long as it "is under control." Teachers who respond in a *dismissing* manner tend to believe that sadness and negative emotions are something the student needs to "get over." They tend to believe that ignoring the behavior associated with the negative emotion will make the emotion go away. Or, they may simply ignore them because they do not see the opportunity as a teachable moment.

Aligned to this, the *dismissing* teacher may feel the need to help the student get over the negative emotion quickly simply for the purpose of moving on to "better things." They work to change the student's sad or angry moments into cheerful ones, to avoid processing with the student regarding the negative emotion. These are the adults who make the argument that expressions of one's feelings serve as a ploy for the student to "get their way." And while observations suggest this may be accurate at times, it serves as a signal that the student has a low EQ and is in need of support to grow in emotional intelligence.

Other observations of *dismissive* responses suggest that the teacher may even believe that negative emotions (e.g., anger and sadness) are harmful or even toxic. As such, these teachers do their best to minimize a student's feelings or to downplay the events that led to the emotion and resulting behavior. By doing so, the teacher inadvertently reinforces the student's misbelief that there is little connection between behaviors and emotion. Such teachers tend to see student problem behaviors as actions void of feelings and circumstances. In their minds, youth is a happy-go-lucky time, not a time to for the worries of the world. Youths have no need to be sad, angry, anxious, or fearful.

One possible reason for such an approach is that these teachers themselves were emotionally wounded as youth. Thus, in their minds, they overcame their circumstances; they "got over it." Wounded adults cannot relate to the vulnerable child they once were (Yerkovich and Yerkovitch, 2017). As such, they do not relate to the vulnerable student standing before them. They have effectively learned to keep personal grief buried, though manifested through anger, depression, and anxiety (Yerkovich and Yerkovitch, 2017). The truth is, there are times where we all have been the victims of such responses by adults. Do you recall a time? How did you feel as a result? How we respond now to student display of emotion is a reflection of the time poured into us by adults in our lives on our emotional growth.

A good set of true/false questions for a teacher to ask to get an understanding of their own personal perspective on this matter is (adapted from Gottman, 1997) as follows:

- When a student gets angry, my goal is to get them to stop.
- For me, there is no need to make a big deal out of student anger or sadness.
- It is hard to take students seriously when they get angry.
- When a student gets angry or is sad, I don't want to hear about it.
- When a student is angry, sad, or disgusted, I believe they need to learn to roll with the punches.
- When a student is angry, sad, or disgusted, I ask, "Why can't they accept the way things are?"

Turning back to the students. Consider the impact of this type of response on the development of your students' emotional intelligence. These are the students who may tend to believe that their emotions are wrong and not valid. They may even believe that there is something wrong with them because of how they feel. In turn, they come to view the negative emotion as the problem, not the resulting inappropriate behavior. This is the student who might be caught saying, "I don't know what is wrong with me," because they had been angry over an issue.

A perspective such as this stunts the student's emotional intelligence development and often leads to them having difficulty understanding, and responding to, emotions in a positive manner. The important thing to remember is that the purpose of growing emotionally intelligent students is to not teach them how to simply regulate or control their emotions, but to help them learn to respond to them in socially acceptable ways. The goal is to help them understand that it is not the emotion that is wrong, but it is when they behave in unacceptable ways. Students who struggle with emotions and are not given opportunities to process them relationally grow to be adults who have similar struggles, ultimately impacting their ability to grow emotionally intimate with others.

The Disapproving Response

For all intents and purposes, the *disapproving* educator response is not much different than that of the *dismissive* one. The key difference is that in this response, the adult understands behaviors in terms of emotions but is quick to judge or criticize the student for expressing emotion and They believe negative emotions simply need to be controlled (Gottman, 1997). Also, in contrast to the *dismissive* response to student display of emotion, the *disapproving* teacher tends to treat a young person's expression of emotion as trivial or unimportant. These adults use phrases like "he/she has issues." The key is to recognize that we all have significant emotional burdens.

Similar to the *dismissive* response, this teacher believes that the student may be using emotions to manipulate the teacher. This often leads to a power struggle in the classroom or school. The focus then is on the student's obedience to authority. The root problem with this approach is the impact on students' understanding of self. Students, who have experienced *disapproving* adults, once again tend to believe that their feelings are not valid (Gottman, 1997). These are the students who have trouble understanding anger and sadness in a positive light. Furthermore, they often feel as if there is something wrong with them because of how they feel. The students see the emotion as what is wrong, not the associated behavior.

Similar to teachers using *dismissive* responses to student display of emotions, these educators do their best to minimize a student's feelings or to downplay the events that led to the emotion and resulting behavior. And as in the previous case, in doing so, the teacher inadvertently reinforces the misbelief that there is little connection between behaviors and emotion in the student's mind. Educators who tend to take this approach to address students' display of emotion tend to believe time-out is a well-deserved consequence for outbursts of anger. Or they simply label a student who is acting out of sadness as a brat.

As with the case of the *dismissive* teacher, these teachers were also most likely emotionally wounded as youth. These teachers tend to believe that since "time out" worked for them, it will continue to do so for future generations. These too are wounded adults that do not relate to the vulnerable child they once were. And, as was the case previously, they do not relate to the vulnerable student standing before them.

Consider your thoughts on the following statements:

- Anger is a dangerous condition for a student to be in.
- Anger is usually a sign of aggression.
- When a student experiences negative emotions, I worry they will develop bad character traits.
- It is not right to display negative emotions.
- When a student is angry, sad, or disgusted, I believe it is an act to get their own way.

• Negative emotions tend to cloud student judgment and they will do something they will later regret.

Once again, consider the impact of this type of response on the development of the student's emotional intelligence. Does the following sound familiar? These students tend to believe that their emotions are wrong and not valid. They may even believe that there is something wrong with them because of how they feel. Like those discussed previously, they come to view the negative emotion as the problem, not the resulting inappropriate behavior. As such, this type of response stunts the student's emotional intelligence development and often leads to them having difficulty understanding, and responding to, emotions in a positive manner.

Reflect on the following: Have you ever been told by another teacher that a student *has issues*? Or, have you ever heard someone tell you that a student is acting in a particular manner simply to get his/her way? What was your reaction? Does it seem a bit misleading to state that a student has issues? By nature, doesn't everyone? It should be argued that any person needs to be able to openly admit that he or she has struggles, especially when they deal with emotions. The key to growing a strong EQ is how we respond when faced with the challenges associated with them. Thus, a good question to consider is: "How can we help the student respond appropriately when they are experiencing negative emotions?" A better question may be: "How can we help the student understand negative emotions in a positive light?"

It is clear that there is a strong intersection between the *disapproving* and the *dismissive* adult. This overlap is most likely due to two key factors: (1) They, themselves, had similar experiences during their formative years in terms of adult responses to their display of emotions; and, (2) they genuinely care for the child and believe they are acting in the student's best interests. It is most likely that these adults find negative emotions overwhelming and, as such, assume the same to be true for the child. Hence, their desire to get the negative emotion to "go away" quickly and to not dwell on the experience. The problem is that these actions are meant to rescue the student rather than help them accept, process, and manage negative feelings (Yerkovich and Yerkovich, 2017).

The end result of well-intentioned interventions is a lack of growth in the student's emotional intelligence. Their EQ is stunted. In an effort to eliminate situations that may lead to tears or pain, they avoid confronting the issue at hand and, in doing so, inadvertently hurt rather than heal. The student is not given the opportunity to experience their emotions and address them effectively. As a result, they enter a world unprepared to face certain life challenges (Gottman). In essence, well-intentioned efforts lead to the suppression of emotions and have a hidden impact on the student later in life.

The Laissez-Faire Response

The third and final of what is considered negative impact approaches is the *laissez-faire* response, or what might be referred to as the *laidback* approach. This style of addressing displays of emotions is in stark contrast to the previous two. Whereas the *disapproving* and *dismissive* teacher rejects displays of emotions, the *laissez-faire* educator openly accepts them. According to Gottman, these are the adults that are filled with empathy (a good thing) for the student and let them know that whatever they are feeling is okay. It is easy to see how one might ask: "How can such a response be considered negative?" Simply put, it is because these are the adults that are "hands-off" about addressing emotions (Gottman, 1997).

While well intentioned, these are the adults who freely accept the emotions regardless of how they are expressed and try to comfort the student when negative emotions are experienced. As a result, while once again unintentional, the teacher fails to help the student understand emotions and at times, accidentally reinforces the negative behaviors that are expressed. Teachers using this approach are those who do not set limits in the classroom, tend to be overly permissive, and do not engage in teaching problem-solving skills. Most often, these are adults who believe that you just need to ride out the situation.

Laissez-faire responses may be displayed in a variety of manners. For example, one teacher may immediately respond to student sadness in a manner that lets the student know they love them no matter what the behavior, appropriate or not, while another believes their role is to comfort an angry student, not teach problem-solving methods and grow emotional intelligence. Teachers who take a *laissez-faire* approach often believe that if there's a lesson to be learned about anger, it is okay to express it (Gottman, 1997).

In opposition to the *disapproving* response, *laissez-faire* teachers often believe that you just need to ride out the situation. According to Gottman, these adults believe that managing emotions is a matter of hydraulics; release the emotion and the work is done. The problem regarding cultivating EQ with this approach is threefold: first, the student does not learn to regulate his or her response to the emotion; second, the student often has a hard time concentrating; and third, the student often ends up having trouble getting along with others and forming friendships. Consider these three thoughts in relation to growing emotionally intelligent students.

Students who have been permitted to freely express emotions openly, without coming to understand how the response impacts those around them, come to believe that it is appropriate to act out in public settings regardless of the circumstance. Consider this example: a student sneaks a peek at her phone during second-hour class (no, this is not about classroom management or students having cell phones in the classroom). The student sees she has a text stating that one of her friends has been in a terrible car crash and is in the hospital. Understandably, the student's immediate response is to cry out loud and "make a big scene" as they say. She cries out uncontrollably.

The teacher, responding with a *laissez-faire* approach, asks her what is going on and upon learning the situation immediately begins to console her, putting aside her class at that time. Again, emphasis is placed here on not evaluating the teacher, rather to contemplate teacher response to display of emotion on student EQ. Also, please do not misunderstand this point, any caring person recognizes that the teacher means well in consoling her student. In fact, it may not be the first time the student has been in a similar situation, hence her comfort in crying out and disrupting the classroom.

However, consider the ramifications of the teacher's response on student EQ. Again, this is not by any means to suggest that a teacher should be unsympathetic. Still, contemplate the ramifications of the *laissez-faire* response in terms of what the student has come to understand about emotions and behaviors. In the student's mind, her actions are not disruptive in that setting as they are justified because she is responding to a negative emotion in a manner now deemed understandable and maybe even appropriate.

At this point, you might ask: "What should the teacher have done?" Part of the answer to this question is addressed later in this book. Suffice to say, the teacher could have considered contacting a counselor to come get the student and follow with a brief dialogue about emotions and behaviors with the remaining students. Often overlooked in growing emotionally intelligent students is how the other students interpret teacher responses. It is understood that the greatest challenge for teachers is found in the limited amount of time with which they can work with students on emotional intelligence development. The pressures of high-stakes testing do not help. However, if teachers are to be successful in their efforts of developing students' emotional intelligence, it will require them to take advantage of opportunities as they arise.

Recall from chapter 2 that emotional intelligence is the ability to respond well to challenges presented by both negative and positive emotions. These challenges may be internal, the emotions we feel personally, or external, the emotions and behaviors demonstrated by others. Either way, teacher response or reaction during such opportunities serves as a tool in the growth of student emotional intelligence.

The Emotion Coaching Approach

The fourth and final approach we discuss is the basis for the remainder of this book. It is what John Gottman refers to as *emotion coaching*. As stated previously, each of the first three responses touched upon thus far can be correlated to having a negative impact on the development of student emotional intelligence. The *emotion coaching* approach is designed to cultivate positive EQ growth. *Emotion coaching*, sometimes referred to as Coaching EQ, uses a process by which the teacher looks at an expression of emotion as an opportunity for openness and an opportunity to process with the other person genuinely and in a trusting manner. While not necessarily a step-by-step process, there are important components of the process.

Through the emotion coaching process, teachers are able to talk with the student regardless of whether the emotion is positive (e.g., happy and gratitude) or negative (e.g., ashamed and haughty) in nature. During this process, it is important that the teacher not get impatient with the student and that they remain respectful of the student's emotions. Teachers who take an *emotion coaching* approach see a student display of negative emotions as a time to help problem-solve. They see such times as an opportunity to help the student explore their emotions and what may mitigate them.

Educators who desire to grow student emotional intelligence through the *emotion coaching* approach understand that it is not only okay but important as well for the student to experience negative emotions. Such experiences serve as a means for the student to discover the things that impact their feelings and how to respond in a positive manner. The *emotion coach* recognizes the need to sit down with the student during such times and talk through their feelings in a safe manner. By providing an open and safe environment to process emotions, the teacher effectively assists the student to discover the "why" simultaneously learning positive social skills. This is an important component of growing the student's EQ.

It is important at this point to note that as part of this process, the educator does not tell students how they should feel and does not try to fix students' problem. This will be discussed in a little more detail later. Suffice for now, *emotion coaching* understands the need for the student to process through the situation. This can be difficult for teachers to do as they prefer to avoid circumstances that are uncomfortable when possible. But, as Dr. Berkowitz (2012a) points out, "Just as weightlifters and bodybuilders claim, 'no pain, no gain,' developmental psychologists can argue that there is no development without conflict and discomfort." And while Dr. Berkowitz is specifically talking about teacher professional development in this case, the same can be said about student emotional intelligence growth.

In contrast to the effects of the three prior approaches discussed, the side benefits of an *emotion coaching* approach are the most desirable. First, and most notably, the student learns to trust not only the teacher but their feelings as well. This is an important piece of the puzzle in the growth and development of student emotional intelligence. Much has already been written on the positive impact of student trust in teachers on academic achievement and other factors (see Gegory and Ripski, 2008; Van Maele and Van Houtte, 2011; Mitchell et al., 2018). Only recently has the student-teacher trust relationship been understood in relation to student growth in EQ.

A second notable benefit of this approach is its impact on the student's self-esteem and self-compassion. In addition to developing a trusting relationship with the teacher, the student develops a sense of high self-esteem and, as such, is more likely to get along with others. As with trusting relationships, much has been written on the importance of student self-esteem. For example, it has been demonstrated repeatedly over time that students with low self-esteem are more at-risk of academic failure than those with a strong sense of self-esteem (see Chambers et al., 2006; Waltz and Bleuer, 1992). Hence, one can see why this is an important side benefit of this approach.

In addition to developing a high self-esteem, the student grows to be more self-compassionate. Instead of always chastising themselves for their mistakes, they learn to be forgiving of their mistakes and failures and to work through times of disappointment and embarrassment. According to Dr. Kristin Neff, associate professor of educational psychology, self-compassion, simply put, is learning to be the warm, supportive friend to ourselves that most of us have. For such reasons, growing student EQ in schooling is equally as important as growing student academic success.

Probably the most important benefit of the *emotion coaching* approach is that the student becomes confident in facing daily challenges and learns how to solve his or her own problems. One of the desired outcomes expressed earlier regarding growing emotionally intelligent students was the ability to respond well to challenges. The ability to problem solve is a key component in that. Though feelings are internal, they most often rise up within us as a result of some external stimulus. Problem solving is the means by which we come to understand these stimuli and work to respond to them in a positive manner. In other words, emotionally intelligent students understand how to process emotions in order to respond to them with socially, and morally, appropriate behaviors.

With all that said, a key question for teachers to consider is: "How would you know if a student trusts you?" Maybe even more importantly: "How would you know if a student trusts their feelings?" How you answer these questions will play a key role in helping you break down any barriers that exist between you and your students and begin the process of assisting them in trusting that their inner feelings are valid. Even more importantly, it helps the student begin to understand that there is nothing wrong with him or her because he or she feels negative emotions.

The simplest way to do a quick recap is to answer the question: "How does an emotion coach view student behaviors and emotions?" Simply put, the emotion coach:

- Sees expression of emotion as an opportunity for developing a trusting relationship with the student.
- Is able to talk with the student regardless of the emotion.
- Does not get impatient with the emotion.
- Respects the student's feelings.
- Does not try to tell the student how they should feel.
- Does not feel they have to fix the student's problems.
- Uses emotional moments to listen to the student, empathize with them, sets limits for expression, and teaches problem-solving skills.

So then, the question remains: "What exactly is emotion coaching?" To answer that question, we start with what it is not. *Emotion coaching* is not a step-by-step process. As stated earlier, it is an approach by which the teacher looks at the problem behavior as an expression of emotion and an opportunity for openness that affords an opportunity to process with the student genuinely and in a trusting manner (Gottman, 1997).

Emotion coaching consists of five skills, which are referred to as habits in this work. These habits are: teaching and building trust (Gottman does not include this step); awareness of emotions; listening with empathy; helping the student label the emotion; and, setting limits and problem solving (Gottman, 1997). Each of these components is intertwined and most often happen simultaneously. Initially, the trust must be built, but often it is an ongoing process. Each of these habits is key in strengthening a student's emotional intelligence. For this reason, we focus on each individually over the next five chapters (figure 5.1).

When Emotion Coaching Is Not Appropriate

Before we go further, it needs be stated emphatically that *emotion coaching* is not appropriate in all circumstances when addressing problem behaviors in

Figure 5.1   The Five Habits.

school. As students move through their days, learning to live in community and deal with daily crises, it seems their lives are wrought with individual challenges. In this context, it must be understood that "*emotion coaching* should not be perceived as a panacea" (Gottman, 1997, p. 127) for every negative emotion and resulting behavior that arises. Even Dr. Gottman (1997) admits that clearly there are situations in which the process of *emotion coaching* a student should be delayed.

Such instances for which *emotion coaching* is not appropriate include the following:

- When the adult is pressed for time
- When there is an audience (it is difficult to build trust and intimacy in public settings)
- When the adult is too upset or too tired for the coaching to be productive
- When the behavior is serious (acts of violence, issues involving the police, etc.)
- And, when the student is actually using the emotion to manipulate the situation

In addition, it should be remembered that not all educators are trained as *emotion coaches* and should not move ahead with incorporating the process without some form of professional development, training, or practice. In addition, for teachers to be successful in implementing an *emotion coaching* approach to addressing problem behaviors, they must believe in the positive nature of human development (Gottman, 1997). Teachers who use such phrases as "he is never going to change," or, "the only thing that is going to change him is time in prison," will more than likely not have a mindset that lends itself to the appropriate application of this process. It is extremely important for teachers to be realistic with themselves and their students.

SUMMARY

If educators are going to nurture the positive development of their students' emotional intelligence and social skills, it will be necessary to reframe traditional school practices that focus on promoting positive behaviors through a discipline system based upon consequences that fail to address the behavior in a redemptive manner. Addressing socially appropriate behaviors can be a complex matter for schools that fail to address the emotional well-being of its students and fail to recognize the power of relationships in the process.

Schools that lack a personal approach to helping students mature both emotionally and socially fail to address root causes of the disruptive behavior.

Relying on positive, trusting relationships, positive role modeling by teachers, and an *emotion coaching* approach to student display of emotions will
greatly increase the likelihood of school success in helping students develop
strong EQs.

The key to all of this is to be aware that student emotional intelligence is
framed by the response of the teacher. Whether the response is positive or
negative in nature, the impact on student EQ growth will be evident. One
need only reflect back on personal experiences to understand the impact each
has. Looking back, it is probably very easy to recall those teachers who were
harsh and cold toward us as easily as it is to identify those who were caring
and compassionate. The question that remains to be addressed is: "How do
you want to be remembered?"

Chapter 6

Habit 1

Cultivating Trust

INTRODUCTION

The goal of this chapter is to begin the process of diving deeper into understanding how the *emotion coaching* approach works and is most effective. During that discussion, it was noted that regardless of the approach we take, we are impacting student emotional intelligence, either in a positive or negative manner. Our response to student display of emotion will directly or indirectly play a role in the growth, or lack thereof, of student emotional intelligence.

In the previous chapter, we identified four responses to student expressions of emotion that impact student EQ. These four responses are directly aligned to the work of Dr. John Gottman in his book *The Heart of Parenting: Raising an Emotionally Intelligent Child.* The first three responses: (1) the *dismissive* response, (2) the *disapproving* response, and (3) the *laissez-faire* response; each has a negative impact on the development of student emotional intelligence. The fourth, *emotion coaching*, has demonstrated to have a positive impact on its growth (figure 6.1).

> "Trust is the glue of life. It's the most essential ingredient in effective communication. It's the foundational principle that holds all relationships."—Stephen Covey

What Do We Mean When We Talk about Trust?

Before we begin any conversation about building and teaching trust, it is important that we develop an understanding of what trust is. There is the Oxford Dictionary definition of trust: "firm belief in the reliability, truth,

Figure 6.1   The Five Habits: Trust.

ability, or strength of someone or something." The Webster Dictionary definition varies only slightly from the Oxford one. It adds: "assured reliance on the character, ability, strength, or truth of someone or something." To this extent, trust is the inner response in which we demonstrate reliance on someone (my parent will provide for me) or something (the chair will hold me when I sit on it).

First and foremost, it is important to remember that when we discuss the concept of trust, we are focused on an emotional response event. To that regard, trust can be logical, something well thought through, or an act of vulnerability, exposing yourself and believing you will not be let down or rejected. Regardless of whether it be someone or something, our trust response is built upon personal experience. For example, I trust my chair will hold me up because it has always done so previously. In my experience, I always had food on the table because my parents provided. But, that is not always the case for all people.

If trust is defined as an emotional response event, then we are compelled to identify those response events most commonly associated with it and with distrust. Signs of trust include a sense of satisfaction, love, a feeling of comfort, friendship, a strong bond with another, and gratitude. Signs of distrust include doubt, anxiety, fear, suspicion, and volatility in a relationship. One reason to focus on teaching trust is that mistrust often leads to a lack of intimacy. To reiterate, intimacy refers to one's ability to fully know and be fully known, without fear of rejection. Suffice it to say, trust is fragile. It can be hard to earn and easily broken. Moreover, it has a big impact on our ability to interact with others.

According to research, trusting relationships are built on four key elements: (1) consistency; (2) compassion; (3) communication; and (4) competency (see Vodicka, 2006). Consistency is easily the most understandable of these elements. It goes back to our previous example of the chair. I trust in the chair because as to date, it has yet to fail me. However, the first time one does, I may be a little hesitant to readily sit down in it again. Similarly, competency is a readily understandable element. If I do not believe someone is capable of performing a task, I do not ask it of them as I do not trust they will be able to complete it.

But what of communication and compassion? What role do they play? After all, I can communicate with someone that I will complete a task, but why should they trust that I will? And how does compassion play into this picture? The following sections seek to answer such questions and lay the foundation for building trusting relationships with, and teaching trust and trustworthiness to, students.

Building Trust

Children who come from homes with an abusive parent do not readily trust adults as those who come from supportive households do. One reason for this is that children who come from such homes had initially put their trust in the offending adult. Once it was broken, it became more difficult for them to trust any adults. Moreover, students who come from such experiences are more likely to be depressed, hurt themselves, be reclusive, bully others, or use drugs. These are the *Tarnished* children referred to earlier. They are less likely to trust teachers but need them desperately to be a source of comfort and support.

If teachers are going to help students grow in emotional intelligence, the first thing they will need to do is recognize that student display of emotion is an opportunity for building trust. More often than not, the teachers' initial reaction to student problem behaviors (understandably so) is punitive in nature. And while timing can present a problem, as well as other limitations, the perspective one takes on this matter is a key starting point. This is not to suggest that there should be no consequences for misbehavior; rather it is to suggest that teachers, and even administrators, need to reframe their perspective on problem behaviors.

Students, especially secondary students who have a history of problem behaviors, have come to expect that educators, in general, will respond to inappropriate behaviors solely with punitive measures as a means for correcting the behavior. As a result, many of these students do not naturally trust their teachers, even if they understand their motives. By reframing their thoughts about how negative emotions are displayed, and subsequently adjusting their initial reactions to problem behaviors, teachers begin the process of taking the relationship to a deeper level and building the trust of their students.

According to Dr. Andrea Bonier (2018), trust is fundamental for a healthy relationship with someone (psychologytoday.com). For emotion coaching to have a positive impact on student emotional intelligence, the teacher-student relationship must be a healthy one. One in which both parties feel free to communicate openly. Hence, building trust serves as a key element in the process. The challenge is that building such trust takes work. The reality is that it is far easier to lose trust than to build it up, due to matters discussed previously. If teachers truly want to play a positive role in the development of student emotional growth, then they will have to be willing to put the effort in.

Before going further with this discussion, it is important to note that the teacher should be aware that the goal is not to fix the student's problems. It is important to remember that one day your students will be promoted, and then eventually graduate, and as such, will not always be able to turn to you for help. Therefore, the teacher must understand that his or her role in the EQ growth process is to work with students in a manner such that students come to an understanding of how to manage their own feelings and respond in a socially appropriate manner. During this process, students come to see their teacher as their ally and come to trust that the teacher is a person with whom they can collaborate together in the future to find ways to manage their emotions better and correct problem behaviors.

In order to accomplish this task, the teacher must be willing to be open, honest, transparent, and even a little vulnerable with their students. By doing so, they model to the student the need for them to respond in a similar fashion. When a student feels secure in the teacher's motives, he or she, in turn, is willing to be open, honest, and vulnerable. This vulnerability allows the relationship to move past the surface level into a deeper understanding and acceptance. This sense of trust creates an opportunity for the student to be open and genuine with the teacher.

Another benefit of being willing to be open and honest is that it helps the student gain a better understanding of respect. Since the definition of respect can vary quite a bit from person to person, for the purposes of this book, definition is defined as "a feeling of deep admiration for someone elicited by their abilities, qualities or achievements" (Oxford English Dictionary). By modeling respect to the student, it is not only the student who benefits but the teacher does as well, by gaining the student's trust and respect.

Dr. Bonier reminds us that a key element in building teacher-student trust is for the teacher to "Say what you mean, and mean what you say." This one is straight forward. Remember the Robert Fulghum quote from chapter 5, "Don't worry that children never listen to you, worry that they are always watching." The truth is you do need to worry that they are listening too. Students expect teachers to carry through with promises made. One of the worst things a teacher can do is commit to something they know they will not be able to see through to the end. It is a surefire way to create distrust. Even students who may be quick to offer forgiveness will have difficulty trusting this teacher in the future. Suffice it to say, choose your words wisely and be willing to commit fully to whatever to say you will do.

Heather Craig (2020), a provisional psychologist at Monash University in Melbourne, Victoria, expounds upon this matter even further. Craig suggests that there are three key components of "Say what you mean, and mean what you say" mantra. The first is simple, think carefully before committing. Don't rush into committing to anything until you have had time to process it carefully and investigate it completely. The second is, if you do commit to do something, make sure to organize the process in order that you may honor the commitment. Some commitments are simple and require very little time and effort. Others though require that the effort be well thought out and organized. And finally, have the courage to say "no."

By nature, most teachers are extremely caring and giving of themselves. A by-product of this is that they are willing to take on any task asked of them for the benefit of another. Many feel obligated to commit to anything asked of them. In their minds, they are simply trying to do "whatever it takes" to help a student succeed. The problem is that there are times when we are unable to complete the task, whether due to inability or lack of time. Be aware of such times and be willing to accept that it is important to do so. Teachers can continue to build trust through saying "no" by being willing to explain any limitations to successfully completing the task—a key component of being transparent, open, and honest. In doing so, they serve as a role model for students who are hesitant to say no.

Before going any further, it is important to note that the process of building trust is a gradual one (Craig, 2020). While many, if not most, early elementary students may come to school with a sense of enthusiasm and complete trust in the teacher, the number dwindles as they progress through the grades. One reason for this is that over time, experiences with adults, not just teachers, have broken their confidence in teachers. This is reflected through a lack of trust and a willingness to be open and transparent with them. As a result, the teacher must be patient and willing to accept the slow going. Teachers should not expect too much too soon (Craig, 2020). In such cases, the teacher must be slow in opening up and being vulnerable with the student so as to not overwhelm them.

One of the challenges teachers face during this trust-building process is knowing when a student does trust in them. One reason for this is that how people display trust is as diverse as how they display emotions. Still, the question must be asked: "What are some specific actions that demonstrate my student trusts me?" Teachers should be encouraged to contemplate this question and even make a list. This is an important step as the possibility remains that even students who may appear cold to a teacher have an underlying trust in them. As students demonstrate manifest behaviors that reflect trust, teachers should be encouraged to use them as a building block upon which to grow an even deeper trusting relationship.

What are some behaviors, actions, or words your students use to manifest that they have trust in you? Make a list here.

How important is it for you to have your students trust you? What are ways you can respond to deepen that trust between you and the student?

Teaching Trust

One could argue that this section is redundant to the previous one. In many senses, that is true as the best form of teaching trust, being trusting as well as trustworthy, is modeling it through the process of building a trusting relationship. The purpose of this section is to encourage teachers to be intentional about the process. As teachers, our efforts to teach academics to students are intentional and well planned. The same can be said about discipline programs and even many character education efforts. Thus, the same should be said about efforts to grow emotionally intelligent students and teaching them how to trust.

For many teachers, conversations centered on the role trust plays in building healthy relationships may feel awkward and uncomfortable. This should come as no surprise as most teacher preparation programs do not build this element into the curriculum. This is due to a number of reasons. The most prevalent is that teaching trust is not seen as a responsibility of the teacher. In society today, the main function of a teacher is considered to be academics, with an added expectation of teaching good behavior.

Referring again to Dr. Bonier's work, we come to understand trust is one of the most crucial building blocks of becoming emotionally intimate with someone. As stated previously, the ability to become emotionally intimate in a positive manner is a vital outcome for growing emotionally intelligent students. Recall that the term "intimacy" as used in this book refers to our ability to fully know another and be fully known by them, without fear of rejection (Wagner and McGee, 2016). For most students and teachers, to seek to fully know another is easy, being fully known is the difficult part. One of the reasons for this is that students are never really taught or shown what a trusting relationship looks like during their academic years. It is an implied construct.

As stated previously, one of the benefits students experience when teachers are willing to be open and honest as part of the trust-building process is that it helps them gain a better understanding of respect. This occurs when teachers take advantage of opportunities to demonstrate to the student that all of us make mistakes, but the important thing is that they learn to act respectfully when they do. By this we mean, being willing to admit our poor choices and make amends rather than trying to mask them or "get out of them." In her book *Dare to Lead*, Dr. Brene Brown refers to this process as the element of *accountability.* Learning this quality is important for later life as we desire to grow emotionally intimate with a significant other.

Patrick Lencioni (2012), in his book *The Advantage*, refers to actions associated with this element as *vulnerability-based* trust (p. 27). According to Lencioni, vulnerability-based trust occurs when we get to a point where we are completely comfortable being transparent, honest, and willing to hide nothing from another person. He adds that this occurs when people are genuinely willing to say "I screwed up" or "I need help." This trust relationship is strengthened when both parties are willing to be vulnerable. This can be exceptionally challenging for teachers, who may feel as if they have more to lose. Thus, "the key ingredient to building trust is not time, it is courage" (Lencioni).

Still, this process also serves as a catalyst in teaching trust. Yet trust is a far more complex matter than being accountable, making it difficult at times for teachers to model and teach. In fact, Dr. Brown's work refers to six other key elements of trust we must understand. In addition to *accountability*, key elements include *boundaries, reliability, vault, integrity, nonjudgment,* and *generosity.* Here is how Dr. Brown summarizes each:

- *Boundaries:* We respect each other's boundaries. When they are not clear, ask. Be willing to say "no."
- *Reliability:* Simply do what you say you will do. Don't over promise. Know your limitations.
- *Vault:* Simply put, don't gossip. Don't share what is not yours to share.
- *Integrity:* Choose courage over comfort. Choose right over fun, fast or easy.
- *Nonjudgment:* We can ask for what we need without feeling judged.
- *Generosity:* You extend the most generous interpretation possible.

Brief conversation has already been given to concepts within the elements of *boundaries* and *reliability.* In addition, the element of *nonjudgment* is embedded in our definition of emotional intimacy. In total, these seven elements serve well as a foundation for teaching students how to trust and become trustworthy. Suffice to say, it is easy to see why teaching and building trust is a complex matter, especially for those students who have endured experiences that have led to distrust of adults. Instead of seeking trusting relationships with adults, they turn to peers and even social media for guidance. While peer relationships are positive in general, there are times when an adult's voice is needed.

Just as understanding intimacy is a complex matter for an emotionally insecure student, so is trust. It is a difficult task to help a wounded student see the importance of trust. George MacDonald, the great Scottish poet and Christian minister, once wrote, "To be trusted is a greater compliment than being loved" (from the Marquis of Lossie, 1877). While no one denies the importance of feeling loved, its power is found in the ability to trust and be trusted. With this in mind, we gain a better understanding of the importance of emotional intimacy.

One means for teachers to overcome any barriers blocking student trust is through actions. It has been said that actions speak louder than words. In the same manner that "students don't care how much you know, until they know how much you care," students won't trust you until they know how much you are trustworthy. People who live in Missouri refer to this as "show me." To put it simply, students will only trust teachers who have demonstrated they are trustworthy.

In the same fashion, teachers must be observant of student behaviors. Through observation of student actions, teachers can get an understanding of those who trust in them, as well as those who are trustworthy. If teachers are to teach students trustworthiness, they must clue into student behaviors and be willing to confront those that are trust breakers, such as sharing confidential information or telling secrets in order to be accepted by a peer. Courage to confront is a key trait in building and teaching trust. The concept of courage here is less about overcoming fears and more about acting on one's convictions despite disapproval. By doing so, teachers model an important character trait for students to understand, taking courage is a means for giving support, confidence, or hope to another (Oxford Languages Dictionary).

As a quick reminder, it is important for the teacher to remember that their role in the emotion coaching process is to work with the student in a manner such that the student comes to an understanding of how to respond in a socially appropriate manner. As such, it is imperative that students come to see the teacher as their ally and someone they can trust as a person. In doing so, the student begins to see the teacher as someone with whom they can collaborate when struggling emotionally. The ultimate goal is to assist the student in developing a high EQ.

The Power of Self-trust

One of the challenges presented to teachers when teaching trust is how well students trust themselves. Self-trust is an often overlooked character trait in the trust-building process. However, before going further with this construct, we should make clear that the concept of self-trust refers to one's firm reliance in their personal integrity (psychologytoday.com). This is where self-trust diverges from confidence, which is reliance in one's ability. According to Linda and Charlie Bloom (2019), a person's self-trust is reflected in the clarity and confidence of his or her choices. Bloom and Bloom further add that persons with a strong self-trust "are interdependent, which includes healthy dependency, not overly dependent or hyper-independent."

For many students, even older high school students, a lack of self-trust is evident. These students tend to lack trust in their decision-making processes and behave in an overly dependent manner on the teacher. Part of the reason for this is the role past events play in the student's current perspective of their abilities. Students whose experiences include consistently being told they could not be trusted or were left to their own devices often fall into this category. They have developed an innate sense that they cannot be trusted to perform a certain task for fear of failure.

While different by definition, self-trust and self-confidence are closely related. To lack trust in oneself immensely impacts one's self-confidence. Students who are often heard saying "I will never be able to" instead of "this may take a lot of work on my behalf" are manifesting not only a lack of self-confidence in abilities but also a self-trust in being able to complete what is being asked of them. Be aware, these are the students who take a self-defeating approach to tasks and circumstances before them, not those who have a healthy understanding of personal limitations. For example, one could recognize they do not have the capacity to run a marathon in under 2.5 hours, but it does not preclude them from trying to complete one.

As one may imagine, student lack of self-trust adds another layer to the complexity of teaching trust. In situations where students lack trust in themselves, teaching self-trust serves as a starting point in building trust. According to Stephen Covey, "The process of building trust is an interesting one, but it begins with yourself, what I call self-trust, and with your own credibility, your own trustworthiness. If you think about it, it's hard to establish trust with others if you can't trust yourself" (franklincovey.com).

So what are teachers supposed to do? How can we begin the process of undoing what many students have endured for years of their life and have readily come to accept as true? The first step is a simple one, one that has been reiterated throughout the book, be a role model. Through modeling that you don't always know all the answers or are not always able to complete a task without help, the student begins to understand limitations from a healthy perspective. It is important to show the student that regardless of an outcome, you always respond in a positive manner. The key is to demonstrate integrity for the student. Integrity that you understand your limitations as well as your capabilities and that you see through to the end, whatever task you choose to undertake.

Another key step in the process is to let the student know that, at times, you question yourself and your abilities. Let them know that it is okay to do so, but to not let such thoughts undermine one's self-trust in seeing the task through to the end. In essence, it is giving the student a picture of the little voice on one shoulder sharing negative thoughts, while the voice on the other shares positive ones and knowing which one to believe. The best way to process this with your student is to help them investigate where the negative thoughts come from and to help him or her confront them in a healthy manner. In other terms, help the student break the chains.

Of course, helping students confront the past in a positive manner is only one of the challenges to the self-trust-building process. Another great challenge for teachers comes from the opposite perspective, fear of the future. According to Bloom and Bloom, there are so many good opportunities all around us that are missed because we are fearful of the possibility of future failure or pain. But, anxiety about what lies ahead is a natural defense mechanism for many students. Their focus on the past leads them to worry about the future. The challenge for the teacher is to get them focused on the present and to believe they have the capacity to achieve good things.

The important thing for teachers to focus on during this process is the student's emotional well-being. Remember, the purpose of any trust-building work is growth in student emotional intelligence. The stronger a student's EQ, the more confident they become and the stronger they grow in self-trust. As students cultivate self-trust, they grow in their understanding of trust and become more capable of building trusting relationships with others.

Rebuilding Trust

We would be remiss if we do not include a brief section on the process of rebuilding trust in a relationship. After all, any teaching on building trust needs to take into account that sometimes the trust we seek to build is one that was broken at some point in the past. It was mentioned earlier that trust is a fragile thing and, as such, can be easily broken. Once broken, rebuilding trust is far more difficult than earning it in the first place. For that reason, we focused first on teaching trustworthiness. Still, what to do if trust is broken.

To begin, it should be noted that although this book refers to trust in terms of emotion, to trust is still a choice we make. Additionally, rebuilding trust needs to be viewed from two perspectives, one from who has been betrayed and another from who has broken trust. Make no mistake, the rebuilding process is an arduous process regardless of which side you are on. The person who feels betrayed, the victim, has little interest in the reason for how it came about. The person who has broken the trust, the offender, knows they have hurt another and may believe there is little they can do to mend the relationship and rebuild trust.

This is where character education plays a big role. Why character education? Because the first step the victim must take is one of empathy. Seeking to understand why a particular action was taken can help break down any barriers put up. This can occur through dialogue. Recall, dialogue is a relational act and a reflective one (Burbules, 1993). The more the victim is open with the offender and willing to listen regardless of how uncomfortable the conversation may be, the better the chance of rebuilding the relationship and trust. Of course, any communication is mute if the victim is unwilling at some point to offer forgiveness. Forgiveness is not easy, but an important step in the healing process.

From the offender's perspective, the first step is in line with the victim's first step, consider why you took the action. Was it simply a mistake or misunderstanding? Or, did you intentionally do something that was meant to hurt someone else. In the same fashion, as the victim must be willing to forgive, the offender must be willing to genuinely seek forgiveness. A sincere apology does not come easily. It means having to admit our flaws. But apologizing is a crucial step toward reconciliation.

The most important thing for both the victim and offender to understand is that the rebuilding process takes time. In addition, it means not dwelling on the past. This is not to say forgive and forget. Forgive, yes. Forget, not necessarily. We learn from the past. The key is not to dwell on it. The most important step, if both parties are truly seeking to heal the relationship, is to commit to the trust rebuilding process. For the teacher, teaching and building trust is challenging in and of itself, walking with students through the trust rebuilding process takes it to another level.

Chapter 7

Habit 2

Awareness of Student Emotions

INTRODUCTION

In the previous chapter, we began diving deeper into the habits of the *emotion coaching* approach. The focus of that chapter was on trust, the foundation for success in this approach. In this chapter, we look at awareness of the student's emotions. Previously, we had discussed the importance of awareness of our own emotions during this process (see chapter 3). As you recall, the five core social and emotional competencies identified by CASEL include *self-awareness.*

While this is an area of growth we want to see in our students, as a teacher, self-awareness of one's own emotions is paramount to effective emotion coaching. We are reminded that power struggles generally arise between teacher and student when the teacher is less aware of his or her own emotions than those of the student. A teacher's awareness of his or her own feelings directly impacts how well he or she tunes into the student's emotions. Remember that students learn by watching, and so an important part of being an effective emotion coach is understanding one's own emotions (figure 7.1).

"When awareness is brought to an emotion, power is brought to your life."—Tara Meyer Robinson

The Second Part of the Process

Having already discussed self-awareness, we move now to a focus on student emotions. The second part of the "awareness" process is that of the specific feelings of the student. The goal is for the teacher to be aware of, and understand, the emotion the student may be feeling for the purpose of helping the

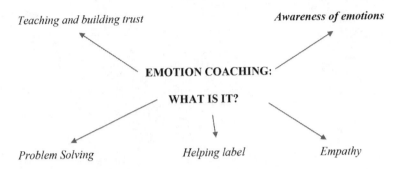

Figure 7.1   The Five Habits: Awareness.

student grow in emotional self-awareness. Dr. Gottman's research revealed that people who are emotionally aware are well equipped for *emotion coaching* (p. 76). What needs to be emphasized here is that awareness of emotions has two key components: the first is being sensitive to the presence of emotions in students, and the second is being able to identify those emotions.

One thing to remember is that emotions manifest themselves in many ways and this can make it tricky when attempting to identify another person's emotions. Two students may not respond the same way to a specific emotion. For example, two students who are angry may not manifest that anger in the same manner. One student may choose to punch something, while the other student yells out at peers while yet another turns red in the face and simply clenches their fists. The prime thing is that the teacher is able to clue into the various behaviors of their students and understand that the behavior indicates an emotional experience the student is feeling.

The ability to identify how a student may be feeling may come somewhat naturally to many teachers. Our research shows that these teachers are most likely to be parents themselves. Just as a parent comes to an awareness of their child's emotions through observations over time, so too is a teacher able to do so. As a teacher comes to know the student better, the teacher, just like a parent, comes to recognize student displays of emotion as just that, an expression of how they are feeling.

There are some inherent challenges for the teacher, however. First and foremost is the number of students a teacher has in the classroom at any one time. While most households average under three children in them, most classrooms average over twenty or even thirty. This has an obvious impact on how well the teacher can get to know each and every student intimately. The second challenge is time. While elementary teachers have a good amount of contact time with their students, middle and high school teachers most often have less than an hour per day. There is also another potential hurdle for teachers, it is possible for one student to feel a positive emotion during an event where another experiences a negative one. A simple example of this case is found in relation to sports. One student reacts jubilantly because a particular team won the game while another is visibly upset. The difficulty here for the teacher is balancing the situation.

Teachers are confronted with any number of formidable challenges in this part of the *emotion coaching* process. While the number of students a teacher has at any one time is a challenge in and of itself, so is the number of varying cultures represented. We touched upon this briefly earlier in this book. In that example, we did not refer specifically to the impact of culture on expression of emotion but response to adults. Suffice to say, the culture in which one is raised has a big impact on expression of emotions as well. For example, research shows that students of Italian and Latino descent are very expressive and passionate, whereas students of Asian and Eastern European descent appear more stoic.

While many challenges to the habit of "awareness" present themselves, they should not be ignored or seen as a barrier that cannot be overcome. Just as a teacher's cultural awareness, sensitivity, and competence are of utmost importance in helping him or her serve a greater community well, the same should hold true for emotional awareness, sensitivity, and competence. The more culturally competent a teacher is, the better he or she is at preparing culturally competent students. Similarly, the more emotionally intelligent a teacher is, the better he or she is at growing emotionally intelligent students.

Teachers should note that being culturally competent, emotionally self-aware, and able to tune into student expression of emotion does not always mean you will find it easy to understand your students' feelings. Gottman found that children often express emotions indirectly and in means that can be puzzling to adults. The key is to listen carefully to the student and try to decode any hidden messages they may be sending. This does not mean all messages they are sending are easy to decipher. Still, alert teachers can gather clues from the actions displayed by their students.

When a teacher suspects a student is experiencing a negative emotion, the first thing he or she will want to consider doing is putting himself or herself in the student's shoes. The more a teacher shares a student's perspective, the easier it becomes in helping him or her process the student's emotions. Still, this can be more challenging than it appears on the surface level. For example, it may be hard for a teacher to have the same perspective as a student who is grieving a loss of something or someone they held dear for the simple reason the teacher simply did not have the same level of connection to that which was loss (e.g., a pet).

Teachers who may have had a similar experience when they were young will be able to relate better to the student's feelings. Still, these teachers will have some difficulty fully connecting in this moment because they have firsthand understanding of how time heals wounds. Something the student has no understanding of at that moment in time. As such, the better part of valor is to share in the pain at that moment but avoiding discussion of future healing until a later time.

Chapter 3 introduced the concept of teachers' self-awareness of their own emotions. As discussed at that time, the teacher's ability to delineate the emotions he or she is feeling is important to the *emotion coaching* process. Teachers who can differentiate between fear and anger in themselves are more likely to be able to do so with their students. Simply put, teachers who understand the subtle differences in the emotions they feel are much more likely to be able to help the student understand these subtle differences as well.

This is not to say that teachers who struggle with self awareness cannot assist their students with this process. Just like the student, it is possible for a teacher to be fully aware of some emotions they are experiencing, such as anger, fear, and hate, while at the same time have difficulty understanding others, such as envy, jealousy, or pride. The important thing to remember is that the emotion growth process is ongoing for both the teacher and the student. Just as teachers model the importance of lifelong learning in regard to knowledge, the same must hold true for emotional intelligence.

The focal point of this chapter is on awareness of student emotion. The bedrock of this habit is found in understanding the differences in experiences between those of the teacher and those of the student. Due to a lack of experience, students are still in the process of understanding their feelings, whereas teachers have had more opportunities to develop a stronger sense of self-awareness. Moreover, the longer the teacher has been out of college, the stronger their sense of awareness will grow.

One final challenge teachers face is how to address students who report no strong sense of emotions one way or another, positive or negative ones. These are the students who lack an understanding of emotions and, as such, are unable to verbalize them. They tend to have a quiet demeanor about them. They may even appear to lack emotions at all. Psychiatrists refer to this inability to recognize or describe one's own emotions as alexithymia.

One caution, because a student does not outwardly display emotions does not imply that they are suffering from this condition. In fact, the symptoms of this condition vary greatly according to psychiatric mental health professionals. Just to name a few, expressions of emptiness, confusion, discomfort, panic, and lack of affection can all be symptoms of alexithymia. It must be reiterated at this time, the purpose of this book is to help the teacher gain a better understanding of growing emotionally intelligent students, not to serve as a means for preparing one to serve as a diagnostician. That is the duty of certified mental health professionals, who some students may already be seeing.

For *emotion coaching* to work effectively, the key is for the teacher to focus on understanding student emotions and the display of them. As stated previously, emotions are a part of all of us. The problem is that some students, and teachers, have difficulty dealing with their emotions, specifically negative ones. So, while some students may suffer from the effects of alexithymia, others may simply repress or suppress negative emotions as a means of avoiding the pain or suffering associated with them.

Students Who Repress or Suppress Emotions

> Unexpressed emotions will never die. They are buried alive and will come forth later in uglier ways.—Sigmund Freud

One of the biggest challenges in this part of the process comes about when students either repress or suppress emotions. The student who represses emotions is unconscious of them and often projects them onto others. These students are unable to communicate the emotion they are feeling simply because they are unaware of it. Needless to say, repressed emotions have a negative impact on the student, not only emotionally but physically, psychologically, and socially as well. Research around repressing emotions suggests that these students tend to be more passive-aggressive in behaviors.

According to Dr. Angelica Attard (2020), emotional repression is all about avoiding emotional suffering. Referring to Dr. M.P. Garssen's work, Dr. Attard iterates that repression can be thought of in terms of a self-defense mechanism. In this sense, the sole purpose of emotional repression is to completely block out negative emotions, or as Dr. Attard refers to it, hide and push away. It is important to note that we all hide our emotions from time to time. Such times occur when we desire to be private about the emotions we are feeling. A person who represses them is taking this process to a higher level.

Previously we touched on the impact of the home environment on our emotional development during our formative years. Students who repress emotions are those who grew up in environments where the expression of emotion was not encouraged or tolerated. They had very little opportunity to discuss how they were feeling, if at all, in a positive manner. For some students, it was openly expressed that displays of emotions were a sign of weakness. For others, the lack of parental, or primary caregiver, displays of emotion led to a belief emotions are to be repressed. Whether intentional or unintentional, invalidated feelings sent one message to the student, "you need to get over it."

As with previous cases, it is important to note that we are not blaming the parent. They are doing their best with the skill set they have. Many of them are simply parenting as they learned through observation. Others want to do "better" than their parents did but simply do not know how. As teachers, the same holds true for us. Raising emotionally intelligent students is not something discussed in our preservice courses. As such, even though we are teachers, if we are also parents, we refer to what we would do as parents. If we are not, we most likely respond as our parents did.

In contrast to repressed emotions, students who suppress emotions do so by trying to ignore them or attempting to escape from them. These students generally display compulsive or impulsive behaviors. They are constantly looking for things that make them happy as a means of escape. Unfortunately, these students are often labeled as having "bad habits" and are easily dismissed and do not get the emotional support they need. There are times where it is appropriate for a student to suppress his or her emotions (e.g., not yelling out in anger during class). As discussed earlier, all of us do it at some point. However, to do so on a continued basis, even when expression of emotion is appropriate, leads to the negative behaviors described earlier.

One of the challenges for teachers when working with students who suppress or repress emotions is determining the reason for the detachment. While we previously iterated that the teacher is not to try and serve as a mental health expert, it is important to determine if some type of trauma or abuse is part of the cause. The teacher is a mandated reporter by law and may be the one adult the student trusts enough to reveal the matter.

What is particularly paramount here is that the teacher be able to clue into behaviors of their students in light of emotions. As stated earlier, this can be challenging as these students do not readily express emotions in an outwardly obvious manner, like punching when angry. As such, these students may be more at risk later in life than those who do. Emotions such as anger, grief, guilt, hate, and jealousy are among the most common. Emotions left unexpressed will eventually manifest themselves in more destructive ways. Anger becomes rage, grief becomes depression, and so forth.

Cluing into signs of repressed or suppressed emotions is of utmost importance for this reason. Clues for teachers to consider, in addition to previously mentioned actions, include such things as changes in mood; a normally talkative student refusing to speak; changing the subject of a discussion; avoidance of tasks or eye contact; the student "fidgets" a lot; the student is lethargic for no apparent reason; and the student says he or she is having struggles sleeping at night. These are only a few of the clues available to teachers. The main thing is for teachers to know their students and be able to identify behaviors that are not generally observed in them.

In such cases, the teacher may want to ask: "Is this student crying out for help?" We must remember that ignoring a student's feelings is not a positive action, and may make the situation worse in the end. We are also reminded that repressing or suppressing emotions is a learned behavior and is usually the result of wanting to be accepted by those around us. These two things are what give the teacher the confidence to work with the student at the lowest level of support. I say the lowest level as to make clear that there is no suggestion the teacher is able to offer the level of support of a trained counselor or psychologist.

It starts with the teacher providing a safe environment for the student to feel free to express the emotion. This will most likely have to occur after all the other students have left as to not cause a disruption, and to give the student a safe space for expression. In older age groups, it may be possible to use class time for this to occur. Check-in meetings (see Berkowitz, 2012a) are a means by which teachers can establish a safe structure for students to openly express themselves on a given topic. They also serve as an excellent opportunity for teachers to become more aware of individual student feelings.

Teachers who serve younger students may choose the use of child-centered play activities that afford students the opportunity to explore and express themselves in a safe manner. Such activities can be used to serve two purposes. First, research demonstrates that they help the student develop a sense of respect and acceptance of self. Second, they allow the teacher to observe the student interacting with others and practicing social skills. These observations can serve as a starting point for conversations that allow the teacher-student relationship to begin moving past the surface level. Through such conversations, the teacher can gain a better awareness of student emotions.

Awareness of emotions is an important component in attending to student feelings. This is particularly important for students that repress or suppress negative emotions. Awareness of the student's feelings gives the teacher the ability to look for opportunities to help the student open up to past hurts. Such opportunities are powerful for both the teacher and student. Students who suffer the effects of unattended wounds most often experience a loss of positive emotions like happiness, joy, gratitude, and even love.

What about Students Who Are Overly Expressive with Emotions?

Let's face it, not everyone came from a home where displays of emotions were discouraged. In fact, many of us came from homes where the opposite was modeled. These are the homes where parents, when angry, let the world know it. Many people who did come from such homes have consciously, or subconsciously, chosen to be less subtle with their displays of emotion. Still, a good many continue with that, which was modeled. The same holds true for many of our students. Yet another example of a student's community impact on their normative behaviors.

In terms of teacher awareness of student emotions, it comes easy here. The student makes everyone aware through their emotional outbreak. One of the challenges presented by overly expressive students is that emotions can be contagious. Though most often subtle, the transmission of emotions is something we encounter on a daily basis, whether we are aware of it or not. According to Dr. Goleman, "We transmit and catch moods from each other in what amounts to a subterranean economy of the psyche in which some encounters are toxic, some nourishing" (p. 114). The challenge for the teacher is managing the impact of such contagion not only on oneself but on other students as well.

Most teachers can readily identify students who impact class culture with their expressions of emotions if not kept in check. Most often, the easiest remedy for dealing with such a student is to simply remove them from the classroom after each occurrence. This serves as an immediate remedy to any disruption of learning in the classroom. While that, in and of itself, is a good thing in the present, without any further interventions aimed at helping the offending student understand their emotions and the impact of such displays, the matter simply repeats itself at a later date.

To combat the recidivism of inappropriate outbursts of emotions, schools may need to rethink their approach to discipline. Consequences alone, while beneficial in the short term, do not help the student grow directly in emotional intelligence, having a more positive impact in the long term. It is only a matter of time before such events repeat themselves, as demonstrated in our example previously about the young man who punched something every time he got angry. Schools need to consider the positive impact of growing emotionally intelligent students on behaviors, as well as on classroom climate and culture.

Refer back to the opening paragraph of this section about homes in which the outward display of emotions, specifically anger, is modeled. An additional problem for schools is that many of these homes serve as a prototype for what it is like to not live in a civil manner. As such, these students present a different challenge in the classroom. Specifically, this challenge has to do with the notion of civility. Students who tend to overly express their emotions in public often do so in inappropriate ways. This more often has to do with a lack of understanding of what it means to act in respectful, responsible, or caring ways.

Addressing such matters can be complex for the teacher. Specifically, the complexity of the matter has to do with terms associated with acting civil (e.g., respectful, responsible, caring, etc.). Even though such terms are defined in modern dictionaries, the actions associated with them can vary from culture to culture, community to community. As a result, the teacher's struggles are not limited to awareness of the student's particular emotion, but in determining the motive as well. Understanding both affords the teacher a better position to help the student grow in emotional intelligence. Yet, when dealing with expressive students, it is somewhat easier for teachers to ascertain the students' motives than their emotions.

Student motive can be readily understood through conversation. Though motives for performing a specific act often vary from person to person, simply asking a few questions gets to the heart of the matter. For example, a teacher may discover how one student may be motivated to get up and come to school each day simply due to a desire to succeed and graduate. Another may do so because of the desire to be part of a sports team; classes are a necessary means to an end. And still a third may come to school because his or her parent forced them; it is the one place they are safe and can be fed. Often, the community or home life of the student plays a direct role on their motive.

This is not to suggest that any one motive is right or wrong, it is merely to demonstrate how motives vary. The problem is when the motive is inappropriate. Consider student motive in the case when two students fight. One student may simply be responding in what can be deemed as self-defense, while the other is doing so as a means of exerting power over the other. We understand and often accept the motive of the student who acted in self-defense, even though we address the behavior. It seems clear how teachers may determine if a student's motive is justified or not. Teachers who do well here will take easily to *emotion coaching.*

For many teachers, it is easy to separate out nuances of addressing behaviors based upon motives. For others, it is a black and white matter. The rules are the rules and students need to be aware of them and to obey them at all times. Codes of conduct reflect this when they reflect that students are to receive the same consequence for fighting regardless of the reason or motive. According to the codes of conduct, this matter is straightforward; fear and hate are similar because they both lead to "bad" behavior.

Yet, consider the duplicity of the matter when emotions are now introduced into the equation. Consider the matter from the student's perspective. These students are baffled by the messages they receive. At home they are told by parents, or even observe actions, that suggest certain negative behaviors are appropriate under certain circumstances. Yet, at school, they receive a consequence for a behavior they consider just. Emotionally, they are perplexed. The perplexity stems from a lack of understanding of the relationship between emotions, motives, and behaviors more than community norms.

Consider what a conversation may look like with the student who was the aggressor earlier. In this case, the administrator was aware of the student's emotion and wanted to dig deeper for clarity:

Administrator: "Do you know why you were sent to my office?"
Student: "Yes, because I got in a fight."

Administrator: "Do you understand that it is inappropriate to fight?"
Student: "Yes."
Administrator: "Why did you fight then?"
Student: "Because he made me mad!"
Administrator: "How did he make you mad?"
Student: "He was showing off his new iPhone"
Administrator: "Why did that make you mad?"
Student: "Because he is always showing off the new things he has that others don't"
Administrator: "Are you mad because you are jealous? You wish you had one?"
Student: "Yeah."

This is a real-life example. Through a short conversation, the educator was able to look deeper, past the motive to the emotion and determine what really was the underlying issue—jealousy. So, while the student may have actually become angry at some point, the true emotion that led to the eventual altercation was jealousy, not anger. As a result of being aware, the administrator was able to begin the process of helping the student understand emotions better.

It is for this reason that schools need to consider discussion around emotions as part of the disciplinary process. It exemplifies the need for students to understand motives and behaviors in terms of emotions. The more students have an opportunity to discuss behaviors in light of emotions, the more likely they are to grow in emotional intelligence. As they begin to understand the impact their feelings have on their motives, and subsequently their behavior, the more capable they become of learning to respond in socially responsible ways to them.

The aforementioned example is a good one for demonstrating how emotions impact motives, though they may differ for two people within one event, yet still resulting in similar behavior. The first student presented most likely would state they were "afraid" or "fearful." These emotions led to the student's motive being self-defense. The behavior was still fighting. The other student may share they were envious or jealous. As a result of these emotions, the student's motive was one of intimidation, leading to an aggressive behavior.

If schools truly seek to focus on restorative discipline practices for addressing problem behaviors, then they must begin by viewing such behaviors through a new lens. Though such efforts can be time-consuming, the reward is worth the effort. As students come to understand the complex relationship between emotions, motives, and behaviors, they begin to grow strong EQs. Fostering such growth requires teachers and administrators to develop an awareness of student emotions and help the student understand these emotions in relation to motivation and actions. Doing so also helps the student development of positive social skills and respond in ways associated with civility.

And What about Civility?

During their college training years, students in teacher certification programs, referred to as preservice teachers, take a course on classroom management. As part of this course, one or two assignments focus on developing a set of classroom expectations or rules. Most often, this assignment culminates in a poster being hung on the wall at the front of the classroom for easy reference. Such practices are good to undertake but are often limited in scope. One such reason for this claim is that a large majority of expectations are listed as what the student is not to do. According to Dr. Philip Vincent:

> It is safe to say that most students are knowledgeable enough of the prohibitions in these codes to have heard or have internalized that "we're not supposed to do that" when confronted by a restricted behavior, even if they engage in it. But knowing what we're *not* supposed to do does not necessarily suggest we know what we *are* supposed to do. Indeed, no one is programmed from birth to use behaviors that are the hallmark of civility—such behaviors are *learned* by observation and practice. (p. 4)

At this point, some may argue that they list student expectations of behavior in terms of positive social skills, such as respect and responsibility. The problem here is that students bring varying interpretations of their meaning. Students need to not only be taught what the teacher's expectation is for actions associated with such terms, but also they must be given the opportunity to practice them. For example, one fifth-grade teacher who listed "respect" as an expectation was observed explaining to students in his classroom that one such action showing respect to others is not talking when someone else is speaking. He emphasized the importance of listening to what the other person had to share. He would remind the students of this practice whenever the need arose.

While the teacher may not have been able to discuss and model every action associated with respect, he did give the students an understanding of what was meant by the term in his classroom. This helped the students who did come from homes where family members talked over each other consistently, and understand how this action was not considered appropriate in his classroom. Remember, civility is not always modeled in the home. Another reason to clearly define expectations associated with certain terms is that they may differ from classroom to classroom, just as they differ from home to home. This can be a source of annoyance for many teachers.

A key finding of research is that a major cause of hateful, angry, rude, and disrespectful behavior is that too many parents are failing to teach positive social skills to their children and failing to offer positive means for expressing emotions. In fact, research suggests that parents and communities actually contribute to problem behavior when they fail to teach the necessary prerequisite social skills and, instead, model inappropriate social interactions.

As such, behaviors that are the antithesis of those describing a civil society appear to be more prevalent in most schools today. It should not be a surprise to anyone that such thoughts come at a time when few schools emphasize the importance of teaching positive social skills and developing emotionally intelligent students. With no specific efforts in place, teachers are left to be creative in finding time and ways to do so.

Consider this matter from the students' perspective. Variance in adult expectations associated with terms such as respect and responsibility can wreak havoc on student emotions. And this variance does not only occur between home and school. Variances in expectations can occur from classroom to classroom. This is most often seen where schools do not have school-level expectations for specific domains. For example, in schools where there is no set policy regarding cell phones in the classroom, one teacher may allow the use of phones during class time, while another may not. Neither teachers should be considered right nor wrong with their expectation, they simply have different expectations that need to be discussed for clarity.

In such cases, it becomes imperative to center discussions on civility as it pertains to the differing expectations. In fact, it may be more of an imperative for the teacher who does permit the use of phones than the one who does not. Research shows that while technology can have a positive impact on student learning, it can have a negative impact on civil behaviors. In addition, it has been demonstrated to have impact on student emotional growth.

The caution for teachers is to not judge a student's motives based solely upon their actions. For example, certain actions readily demonstrate when a student is acting in a "caring" fashion, but does not acting in a specific manner mean that the student is "not caring"? Or, if a student does not complete his or her homework, does that imply they are not "acting responsibly"? The same holds true for emotions. One person may interpret a student's particular behavior as acting in an "angry" manner, but does it necessarily mean the student is indeed so? The teacher who has a good understanding of his or her students in such cases is better prepared to serve as an *emotion coach*.

Teaching positive social skills and growing emotionally intelligent children has come to fall on schools. In fact, such goals have become a necessity in today's classrooms. Teachers can be assured that through the process of growing emotionally intelligent students, the student learns positive social skills and how to behave respectfully, politely, and courteously in communal settings. It is imperative that schools embrace this role and come to see it as vital. They must embrace the responsibility of developing students, not just in terms of academics but socially and emotionally as well. Awareness of student emotions is a good starting point.

Chapter 8

Habit 3

Listening with Empathy

WHAT MORE CAN BE SAID ABOUT EMPATHY?

You may be thinking at this point, what more can be written about empathy. A simple search on Google of the word "empathy" produces almost 158,000,000 results. It has become a buzzword in education and there is a plethora of material available about it. Searching "empathy and education" on Google still produces over 110,000,000 results. True. The goal of this chapter is not to expose you to anything you may not already know, but to get you thinking about the role of empathy in growing student emotional intelligence. Specifically, listening with empathy.

According to both Goleman and Gottman, empathy is one of the key components for helping grow the emotional intelligence of children. Goleman refers to empathy as "the fundamental people skill" (p. 43). Gottman talks about it as "the foundation of *emotion coaching*" (p. 70). And while this book lists it as Habit #3, it in no way lessens the importance of it. One only need recall that the first three habits are not in any sequential order or ranked importance. They are interwoven and only segmented out for clarity of purpose. Suffice it to say, if teachers are to take student growth in emotional intelligence seriously, they must look at student behavior from a different perspective, from one of empathy (figure 8.1).

"If we share our story with someone who responds with empathy and understanding, shame cannot survive."—Brene Brown (in *Daring Greatly*)

Figure 8.1   The Five Habits: Empathy.

Understanding Empathy

One of the interesting things to consider during any discussion on empathy is that not only is it a means of responding to another person but, in and of itself, it is an emotion as well. Therefore, it becomes necessary for us to first define the term as this book refers to its use. According to *Psychology Today* (n.d.), empathy is "the experience of understanding another person's condition from their perspective; the ability to place oneself in another's shoes." This book adds to that definition to include "it is the ability to accept another's feelings without judgment." To that effect, empathy can be defined more simply as understanding others and taking an active interest in their concerns (globalleadershipfoundation.com).

Over the years, many companies have spent countless hours on research in order to develop tools aimed at measuring one's emotional intelligence. Such tests have been shown to be effective in giving one a deeper understanding of self. However, the extent to which they can specifically measure one's level of empathy is another matter. To that end, one may want to try Goleman's test for measuring one's level of empathy.

Daniel Goleman suggests that a good test for evaluating one's empathy level is to have them read a person's feelings through their facial expressions. Doing so gives a picture of one's ability to look past a person's outward appearance into a deeper part of their being. While mostly unintentional, teachers are expected to do this on a daily basis. And most do so unintentionally. The goal here is to make it an intentional habit.

Learning to read the faces of our students may come easily to many but responding to them empathetically can be a challenge at times. This is especially true when working with younger children than one may realize. Earlier in the book, we gave good examples of approaches some take that do not include empathy toward the student. One such example, the *dismissive* teacher, may tell a young child "life's not fair" or "you should be happy with what you have" when the student is jealous because their friend has something they do not have but have wanted.

In his or her mind, the teacher may actually be well intentioned in such comments, believing they are getting the student to look at life from a more positive or realistic perspective. Yet, the reality is that the student's emotions are completely dismissed. The more this happens, the more the student comes to believe their emotions are invalid. We inadvertently invalidate the child's feelings.

The irony is that this same teacher may be one who responds empathetically to another adult in a similar situation. Instead of stating "you should be happy with what you have," they respond with "Yeah, it would be nice to have something like that." By doing so, the adult's feelings are validated. Hence, teachers need to be cautious with their responses. They must avoid the temptation to redirect the student's feelings and inadvertently discount them. We must remind ourselves that students are still in the process of learning about emotions and have had fewer life experiences from which to gain understanding.

As teachers, we must come to understand empathy as the ability to see the situation from the perspective of the student. While our personal experiences inform us and provide wisdom about how life events may possibly play out, we must not allow them to influence our responses to our students. Think of empathy in terms of walking beside the student, affording him or her the opportunity to work through life's experiences while we serve as a means of support and encouragement. This is especially true in cases where it means working through pains associated with negative emotions. Remember, one goal of *emotion coaching* is to validate the feelings of the student. This serves as a starting point for helping the student develop a strong EQ.

Research shows that empathy is an integral part of any trusting relationship. Students who sense empathy in a teacher's response to their feelings show a greater level of trust and security in that person. Results such as these not only benefit the student but the teacher as well. As the student begins to feel validated and accepted, and begins to trust the teacher more, the teacher gains a higher sense of satisfaction in his or her efforts. A higher sense of satisfaction builds the teacher's confidence and conviction that he or she is making a difference.

With such a positive impact, it is understandable why Dr. Steve Taylor states that "empathy is one of human being's highest qualities." Taylor further states that "empathy is the root of most behavior that we associate with *goodness*." Bearing that in mind, one could argue that current events associated with racial injustice and political polarity are a reflection of a lack of empathy in our society today. We no longer seek to see things from other's perspectives. Such a lack of empathy leads to what Taylor refers to as "the root of most destructive and violent behavior."

Consider such strong words when working with students. Many of the disciplinary problems we witness in schools today may be tied to students who have never been shown empathy in their formative years. Most often such frustrations manifest themselves through aggressive acts such as fighting or breaking things. In extreme cases, such students take their aggression to a higher level. This is not to suggest that empathy is all that is needed to stop violence in schools. What is being suggested is that students who do not experience empathy as part of their emotional development are more likely to act out more aggressively than those who do.

Research reveals that students who do not experience empathy during their formative years tend to feel more mistreated and unwelcome than others. Immediately, one quote that comes to mind when thinking of mistreated beings is from a fictional book by Alice Hoffman titled *Magic Lessons: The Prequel to Practical Magic.* One character in the book, Maria, determines to set a captured wolf free. Another, Samuel warns her to be careful, it is a dangerous creature. Maria replies, "Every mistreated creature is dangerous" (p. 211).

The same may hold true for students who we are cautioned about, the tarnished students previously mentioned who have experienced many of life's difficulties from an early age. They see themselves as having been mistreated in life. Most often, their desire is simply to be understood and accepted. Overtime, if not provided these opportunities, they can grow to be dangerous, to themselves or others. Empathy toward the mistreated can serve as a starting point for helping them feel accepted.

The big question then is: "Can someone develop empathy or is it something we have innately?" The answer according to social scientists is both. To some extent, human beings are designed to empathize with others naturally. A good example of this is when we are sad or cry because someone else is sad or crying. Though this may not be true of everyone, at times we all directly connect with someone else's joy or pain in some fashion. Some teachers do it better than others. It comes more naturally for them. These are the teachers who can pick up on someone's feelings just through observation of facial expressions.

By contrast, others need to work at it a little. These are the teachers who do not sense someone is angry until they either yell or hit something or someone. This does not imply they are unempathetic. There is still some level of empathy within, it is just at a smaller level. As such, they have to work harder at being empathetic. The reality is most teachers fall somewhere in between. They can get a read on a student's feelings but have to work at listening and responding with empathy. It is for this group that the book discusses self-awareness early.

The best means for understanding the emotions of others is through understanding our own. Just as with self-compassion, the more we can empathize with ourselves (understand and accept our own emotions), the better we will be at empathizing with others (listening and relating to their feelings). The more we are comfortable with who we are and value that, the better we are able to empathize with students.

Listening with Empathy

"When a quiet man speaks, listen."—Mike Greenberg (on *GET UP*)

As demonstrated earlier, a teacher's ability to show empathy toward a student is vital to success in any *emotion coaching* effort. It is a foundational component of growing emotionally intelligent students. The more we show empathy, the more students understand it and, in turn, begin to embrace it as a personal character trait. Showing empathy is one thing, but what is meant by listening with empathy?

The first thing to be reminded of whenever the topic of listening is considered is that there are two persons involved. The first is the one listening with empathy, the teacher. The second is the one being empathized with, the student. Because listening with empathy is relational, there exist three key components to it: (1) communication interactions, (2) student perception, and (3) student response/reaction. These elements are sequential, how well each individual component plays out directly impacts the one that follows. In this case, the onus falls on the teacher, as listening with empathy is the goal.

In this three-step process, communication interaction from the student's perspective refers to a willingness to share openly, honestly, and as transparently as possible. Hence, trust plays a vital role. A trusting relationship is the basis for each student being willing to share to the extent that they make themselves vulnerable. From the teacher's perspective, communication interaction simply refers to showing interest in what the student is sharing by being attentive each moment and not thinking about what to say next. It involves attending to the student's needs by listening for emotions that may be underneath the surface of what is being shared.

Teacher actions that demonstrate listening with empathy include validating the student's feelings, showing appreciation for trusting you as a confidant, and showing a genuine concern for the student. While all three of these actions can be completed verbally, it is important to note that empathy can be nonverbal as well. This is achieved through our facial expressions and body language. In essence, the student can understand what we are thinking or feeling through our expressions.

It is important for the teacher to be transparent as part of listening with empathy. Be honest with the student. Sometimes a student may come to you at a time when you are not able to fully attend to them. It is possible you have a meeting that you absolutely cannot miss or arrive too late. Or, maybe they come to you during class. Inform the student you would love to talk with them when you can give them your full time and attention.

Delaying talking to the student can present a challenge as they may be coming to you at a time when they need someone most. In such cases, it is worth asking the student if there is someone else he or she may be willing to talk with. Do not be offended if the student is okay speaking with someone else. Often, many people are involved in the student's life who have a vested interest in their growth and well-being. It is good to have a team or support group in place.

Still, it may be a case where he or she would rather wait to speak to you. Remember, this is someone with whom you have built a trusting relationship. If it does not appear to be an emergency (most cases are not) ask if you can speak with him or her later. If it is an emergency, then referring him or her to the appropriate adult is justified. In such cases where you are the best person for addressing the matter, it would warrant you being excused from your meeting. Teachers and administrators understand the importance of putting student needs first.

The thing to remember most when we talk about the interaction phase is to think in terms of how you would want someone to respond to you. Students desire that same response. They seek to be listened to in the same manner you do. And be careful of your facial expressions and body language. If you keep looking at the clock because you have somewhere to go, you are not interacting in a manner deemed as listening with empathy. The key is to be present at all times and listen.

The second step of the process, perception, refers to how much the student perceives you care and is acting empathetically toward them. If the student does not perceive you as listening with empathy, then your actions are not empathetic. In order for the student to perceive that you are listening with empathy, you must be engrossed in the conversation. Being fully engaged means that the teacher puts aside their own desires, needs, and opinions to attend to those of the students. Through fully attending to the student's words, the teacher is perceived as being empathetic to their situation and has a better perception of the interaction.

The third and final step in the process is the student's response or reaction. If the student believes that the teacher is listening with empathy, he or she will respond in a positive manner. In some cases, the student may feel so good about the interaction that has taken place, that he or she too begins to listen to others with empathy. When this happens, we are reminded that, as teachers, we serve as a bridge to learning on more than just an academic level.

Ultimately, if all goes as hoped, both teacher and student feel good about the process. Students feel heard and understood. They feel as though they have a voice. They come to see the teacher as understanding and caring. They see the teacher as not only caring "about" them but caring "for" them as well. This is because the teacher has helped them meet a need. As such, they trust the teacher even more. Their admiration for the teacher grows even stronger.

From the teacher's perspective, the student feels rewarded for his or her efforts. There is a sense of satisfaction, a sense of achieving a goal. As a teacher, there is a sense of pride in knowing you are having a positive impact on your student's growth in emotional intelligence. In this, the process has a positive impact on the teacher's emotional state. They come to trust the process more.

It is understandable that the outcomes of the listening process are positive when empathy is applied to it. But, we need to be reminded that lack of empathy during the communication process can have an extremely negative effect. Similar to the impact of the *disapproving* or *dismissing* approaches discussed previously in this book, the student may believe that their emotions are invalid. They believe their feelings are what is wrong or that there is something wrong with them because of how they feel. They have difficulty regulating emotions. The student may even see the teacher as uncaring or see oneself as a nuisance.

And what about the *laissez-faire* approach? On the surface, the *laissez-faire* adult appears to listen with empathy, but it is something quite different. The *laissez-faire* adult listens with sympathy, it is quite different. In this approach, the adult listens to the student but tends to be overly permissive and is focused more on offering comfort than teaching about emotions. If you recall, this approach leads to the student having difficulty regulating their emotions and having a hard time concentrating. They may even have a hard time getting along with others.

To be clear, this is not to suggest that sympathy is a bad thing or wrong. And I am not suggesting that one be unsympathetic. This is simply to point out that there is a difference between listening with empathy and responding with sympathy. While both are signs of caring, the difference in impact on efforts to grow student EQ is vastly different. And to reiterate, this book defines sympathy as a feeling of pity or sorrow for someone else's misfortune.

Empathy versus Sympathy: What Difference Does It Make?

The first thing to make clear, prior to going any further, is that there is a time for both empathy and sympathy when working with students. I am certainly not suggesting that it is wrong to show sympathy toward students. The purpose of this section is to address the issue in terms of *emotion coaching* and growing emotionally intelligent students. There is a marked difference in the impact of each approach on student growth in emotional intelligence. Thus, the goal of this section is to demonstrate the difference.

First and foremost, listening with empathy achieves an important goal of *emotion coaching*; it validates the student's emotions, not necessarily the behavior. To reiterate, one of the key goals of growing emotionally intelligent students is that they come to understand behaviors in light of emotions and learn to regulate them accordingly. The focus is on helping students develop positive social skills through the process of understanding the impact emotions have on our actions.

This is somewhat in stark contrast to a sympathetic approach. To get a better understanding, let us take a deeper look at the key difference between the two and why empathy is the recommended approach. Consider figure 8.2. On the left, the person showing sympathy is comforting the other during a rainy period in life. In fact, the person is actually experiencing the rain with the other. Certainly, one feels the care and support of the other. However, the problem is not solved as the person continues to get wet. In fact, in this case scenario, both do (figure 8.2).

Now consider the image on the right. In it, empathy is defined as helping another overcome the difficult issues they encounter. It is a means of offering

Sympathy   Empathy

Figure 8.2 Sympathy and Empathy. Source: *dreamstime.com: ID 28262713 © Corina Rosu & ID 33716361 © Ribah2012 https://www.dreamstime.com/stock-photos-friends-image28262713, https://www.dreamstime.com/stock-image-d-people-under-black-umbrella-illustration-two-person-rendering-man-character-image33716361*

not just comfort but support as well. As a result, the person struggling not only comes to understand the benefit of the umbrella but experiences it as well. In fact, as suggested previously, both benefit from the effort. Neither one is getting wet.

This example may be oversimplified, but it gets the general point across. Sympathy is a good practice for comforting a hurting student. Whereas empathy is a good practice for helping the student find solutions to their struggles. Again, each has its place when working with students, particularly younger ones; however, empathy is better in the process of growing emotional intelligence. Maybe this point will be better reflected through the following real-life scenario:

A female high school student has been given permission to leave school early one day for personal reasons. She has a car and drives herself to and from school. Just outside the school parking lot, she found herself in a fender bender with an unattended parked car. She was not hurt physically, but she became emotionally distraught. Her immediate response was to seek a teacher with whom she has developed a trusted relationship.

The problem is that the teacher was teaching her third-period class at that moment in time. Without hesitation, the student, in tears, burst into the room seeking the comfort of the teacher. The teacher, responding as most sympathetic adults would, reached out to the student without delay to comfort her. She hugged the student and told her everything was okay. The student eventually calmed down and shared with the teacher what had happened and how she had left her car where it was to find her. The teacher again reiterated she understood why the student had responded as such and told her it was okay.

Herein lie two problems with the teacher's response in this situation: the first has to do with the message the student received—it is ok to interrupt or be disruptive when you find yourself emotionally upset; and the second is the message the class received—it is ok to interrupt or be disruptive when you find yourself emotionally upset. The issue here is not the disruption of learning, it is the subliminal messages being sent. There is no disagreement that the teacher needed to address the matter, as it was a delicate one. However, the difference in messages sent between the sympathetic approach utilized in this case and the empathetic approach suggested further is significant.

The sympathetic approach gave the student the sense that the way she had acted was acceptable, thus, can be applied to future circumstances. In fact, all the students in the class at the time could come to the same conclusion. It also communicated to both the student and the class that the expression of emotions in this manner, not just in the context of school but in general, is appropriate. Not only is this harmful to the classroom setting, but consider how it will also likely impact the student's behavior in the workplace and family context.

Contrast that to an "empathetic" approach. The empathetic approach is one in which the teacher works to move the student to another setting and tells the student, "I understand you are facing challenges right now, let's process the situation elsewhere and discuss a better approach on how to react to this type of situation in the future." Remember, be open with the student about when or where is the right time to process such events. The message in an empathetic approach is clear: it is the behavior that is inappropriate, not the emotion.

It is very probable that as an individual, you have had an emotional experience similar to that which the student encountered. Such experiences result in your ability to relate to the student on a personal level. This helps you in (1) processing the situation with the student; (2) offering comfort and an empathetic ear in an appropriate setting; and, (3) validating the student's emotions while addressing the behavior. In cases where we have not experienced similar situations, the teacher can validate the student's feelings by using such statements as, "I probably would have felt the same" or "that must have been frightening."

Admittedly, this example is representative of rare and extreme cases. It also exposes a different challenge for schools. The teacher was not permitted to leave the classroom unattended even knowing it was in the student's best interest. This is understandable, as it is a matter of safety for the other students. Yet, teachers often address problems in the classroom by referring students to an administrator or counselors to assist in the matter. In this example, that is the recommended approach, even if for no other reason to de-escalate the student's emotional state. Then a follow-up discussion between student and teacher, at an appropriate time and location, could take place.

One final point as we come to the end of this chapter. Due to the potential negative outcomes of not listening with empathy (taking a *dismissive*, *disapproving*, or *laissez-faire* approach), each teacher should complete a self-audit of one's capabilities and expertise in this realm.

> How good are you at validating a student's feelings?
> How well do you show appreciation for the student trusting you as a confidant?
> How well do you demonstrate a genuine concern for your students?
> What skills and qualities do you possess in regard to listening with empathy?

This habit, indeed the entire *emotion coaching* process, should not be taken lightly. Not everyone possesses the qualities to be good at it. In the same manner, one has to study to be smarter or practice to be better at a particular sport, listening with empathy requires reflection, study and, most importantly, practice. Practice with your spouse or boy/girlfriend (a very good idea), your child(ren) (also a very good idea), a friend, or even with students in a low-intensity situation. Ask for feedback on how well you are doing. The more confident you grow in your ability to listen with empathy, the better you are able to use it during conversations with students during times of intense emotions.

With everything now said, it is easy to see why there is a plethora of material available about empathy and the power it has on growing emotionally intelligent students. Research demonstrates that teachers who listen with empathy as part of the *emotion coaching* process have students who are better off academically, socially, physically, and emotionally. Thus, schools that support the flourishing of youth (academically, socially, and emotionally) prioritize such practices as the use of empathy as an integral part of shaping their student's development.

Chapter 9

Habit 4

Labeling Emotions

INTRODUCTION

So now we reach the fourth habit of the *emotion coaching* process, helping students put words to their emotions. While probably the easiest of the five habits, it is one of extreme importance. One of the biggest barriers for students to their emotional intelligence development is an inability to define which emotion they may be experiencing at a given time. As adults, we take this for granted. Years of experience have helped us understand better when we are feeling sad, happy, or angry. The same cannot always be said for our students. In fact, it is the years of experiences we have had with our feelings that allow us as teachers to empathize with our students.

It is not uncommon for a teacher to look at a student's facial expressions and state "you look angry, are you mad about something?" Most teachers seem instinctively programmed to recognize when a student is angry, sad, or happy. That is what gives us our ability to empathize. But we must reiterate here, labeling the emotion is not telling the student how they should feel. It is helping them put a label to the feeling (figure 9.1).

"Labeling your emotions provides useful information"—Dr. Susan David (in *Emotional Agility*)

Labeling versus Telling

Helping label an emotion can be a complex matter. What makes it complex, as stated previously, is the reality that two people do not always act in the same manner in response to a specific emotion. That is because expression of emotion is a complex matter involving a number of variables, including

Teaching and building trust   *Awareness of emotions*

EMOTION COACHING:

WHAT IS IT?

Problem Solving   ***Helping label***   *Empathy*

Figure 9.1.   The Five Habits: Helping label.

but not limited to: setting in which the event occurs, cultural norms, and the person's mood and personality type. Hence, determining the specific emotion a student is feeling requires a complex process of integrating knowledge of these variables as they apply to an individual student.

Since helping label emotions can be challenging at times, there exists a temptation for the teacher to tell the student what they are feeling. Statements like "you are sad" or "it is clear you are angry" may be well intentioned, however, are not to be considered in the labeling process. The goal of this habit is to help the student identify the emotion associated with the way they are feeling. This is an important step if the goal is to help the student grow their emotional intelligence. Thus, telling a student the emotion he or she is feeling may help work through circumstances in the moment, but it does not help achieve the long-term goal.

The key to this habit is for the teacher to help the student put words to the emotion. Rather than making statements, the teacher should consider asking questions that help reveal what emotion the student is feeling. Questions such as "how did that make you feel" and "how do you feel about that" start the reflection process for the student. In some cases, the student may need a little more direction. In such cases, questions like "are you feeling sad," "that appeared to bother you, did it," or "you appear to be upset, is that how you feel" help the student get started with the reflection process.

With younger students, it may be necessary for the teacher to take it a step further as they are still in the foundational stages of their emotional development. In such instances, the teacher may use statements instead of questions. The key is to phrase the statement in a manner that leads to introspection by the student. "You look pretty sad," "It appears that you are upset," or "you seem worried" give a young student a starting point for identifying their feelings. Often the student will respond in agreement, but there will be times where they do not. It is not uncommon for a student to respond in the following manner, "I am not worried, I am just upset." This opens the door for a fruitful conversation.

One reason for the teacher assessing the emotion one way and the student another is that sometimes, the student's feelings change during an event. We tend to refer to this as "mixed emotions." As such, teachers should be prepared to make room for mixed feelings. Mixed emotions add another layer to the challenge of helping a student label the emotion. Due to the duplicity of emotions, the student may have difficulty determining which one he is feeling at a given moment. For example, the student may have initially been frightened by an event but then grew to be angry. As a result, they go back and forth between the two during this part of the discussion. It is important for the student to understand both feelings.

While conducting research for this book, interviews revealed that there were two emotions students tended to intertwine with each other. Any guesses as to which two emotions students most often mix together? If you said anger and fear, you are correct. On numerous occasions students stated that they were angry at the time they had acted out, but after processing the situation more, determined it was fear that they initially felt. Why might that be? Consider the following scenario:

A teacher brings a high school student to the office after he/she punched another student in the hallway. The teacher informs the principal that he saw the two students interacting in a hostile manner toward each other but before he could get between the two, one had punched the other in the head. In order to best address this issue with the offending student, the principal asks a series of questions to get a better understanding as to why the student acted aggressively and to determine the best course of action for helping the student deal with similar situations in the future.

While processing the sequence of events, the principal ascertains from the student that the other student had said something to him first and had approached him in an aggressive fashion. When asked how he had felt about that, the student responded that he had felt angry and, as such, punched the other student. Seeking further clarification, the principal asks the student if it was what the other student had said to him that made him angry or the aggressive posture taken. The young man responded that when the other student had approached him in a particular manner, he felt unsafe and that his reaction was more in self-defense.

Asked to put a name to the emotion he was feeling, he stated "anger" basing his decision on the fact he had punched someone. However, careful reflection revealed the young man was more in "fear" for his safety than actually angry, at least initially. This is an important point to clarify with the student. The better students understand how particular emotions make them feel at a given moment, the better they will be able to develop appropriate response behaviors to them.

This example exposes a challenge for teachers. In this scenario, the student found himself in "fight or flight" mode. It is an innate mode in humans. In this case, the student's natural response code was "fight." Over time, as the student's EQ grew, he came to understand his feelings better and realized that not responding in an aggressive manner actually de-escalated tense situations he found himself in, allowing him to walk away (flight) without any exchange of physical aggression.

Research has demonstrated that when people do not understand their emotions and learn to respond to them in an appropriate manner, they tend to exhibit a lower sense of well-being and have more physical symptoms associated with poor health. Similarly, students who struggle emotionally tend to suffer from higher levels of stress. When students are not afforded the opportunity to address their emotions, specifically negative ones, they tend to try and avoid them. And as demonstrated previously, there is a high cost associated with avoiding one's feelings.

This points to the fact that putting words to feelings matters. Students who experience strong emotions need to be given the opportunity to reflect and name them. The more opportunities given, the deeper the student's understanding of emotions and the broader their vocabulary of emotions becomes. Younger students tend to use broad categories to define emotions, for example, angry, sad, afraid, or embarrassed. The older they get and the more opportunity the student gets to process emotions, the more they understand varying levels of such terms. For example, anger can be subcategorized further using such terms as "annoyed" or "irritated" to display being somewhat angered, versus "furious" or "livid" to display extreme senses of anger.

One of the goals of *emotion coaching* and the helping label habit is to assist students not only in putting words to feelings, but in understanding the varying levels of them. This is important as students are very likely to use stronger variants in describing an emotion even when the feeling is less extreme. A conversation with a student may include words such as "dismayed" or "depressed" from the student but eventually lead to a lesser level such as "disappointment." The flip side can be true as well. Students may choose to use a word such as "hurt" to describe the feeling because they are not familiar with the idea of being victimized or aggrieved. This is especially true in younger students.

Understanding the Intensity Levels of Emotion

Helping students grow in their vocabulary of emotions is an important growth component of emotional intelligence. Even more important is understanding the varying levels of the emotions they feel. Students are often surprised by the span of their emotions. They become even more surprised when the labeling process helps them uncover deeper emotions hidden by the limited understanding of levels of feelings and the corresponding vocabulary. This is why helping label is a key habit in the *emotion coaching* process. It is also why it is important for teachers to familiarize themselves with the varying levels and breadth of vocabulary terms.

As important as it is to help the student broaden their vocabulary of emotions, it is equally important for the teacher. By broadening their vocabulary, teachers can help students label and understand their positive and negative emotions on more specific levels of intensity. This is important as two students who use terms such as "good" or "happy" to express their feelings may be at different levels of emotion. One may be content while another is elated. Having a strong EQ requires understanding levels of emotions from both ends of the spectrum.

One of the practices we find helpful during the labeling process is to have the student use multiple terms to define how they feel. After a student has stated his or her initial response, ask him or her to use another term to express how he or she feels. For example, suppose a student has shared that he or she is feeling anxious, see if he or she can identify another term to describe the level of anxiety he or she is feeling. The hope is that the student will reveal which end of the spectrum the level of anxiety is. Are they simply worried or are they panicked? A student who has an understanding of the varying levels of an emotion, tends to have a more well-developed emotional intelligence.

Some students may struggle with finding an alternative term. This is okay. In such times, it will be necessary to assist the student with finding alternative terms. For example, the teacher may choose to ask: "Were you nervous, or afraid?" Explain to them that you are trying to determine the level of anxiousness. This helps the student start to understand the varying levels of an emotion.

The key is to be judicious during this step of the process. This is a delicate matter; you want to do it in a manner that does not make the student think you are questioning how they feel. The goal is to dig deeper in order to help the student recognize the different levels of an emotion. As such, when a student expresses he is "afraid," a response like "That does sound horrifying, is that how you feel?" will be more beneficial to achieving that goal than a comment such as "Are you afraid or is it something else?" The process of using a second term to determine the level of intensity helps both the teacher and the student. The teacher is able to more accurately evaluate the situation. The student has an opportunity to more accurately pinpoint the emotion.

Remember, this is a time when students are vulnerable. How transparent they are reflects the level of trust that has been established. You do not want to break that trust. It is important to note, at this time, that just because a student is willing to discuss their feelings with a teacher, does not imply a trust bond. We have observed students who were willing to share, on a surface level, with a teacher because he or she was "nice," but when they stated that they "trusted" the teacher, we observed a willingness to go deeper, into the level of emotion they were experiencing. This is especially true when talking about negative emotions such as fear, hate, grief, and anger. The deeper the conversation, the greater the trust revealed.

And that leads to another important discussion with students; understanding when it is a matter of trust with what they share versus simply being comfortable doing so. The world of social media may be impacting this distinction more than we realize. Students have become more open to sharing personal matters with multitudes through social media platforms. This seems to be in stark contrast to when the primary source of communication is face to face. In seeking "likes" or other sorts of positive reinforcement through what has been posted, they lose sight of the fact that they are not impervious to the counter effects of doing so. Negative experiences on social media have been demonstrated to have a direct negative impact on a student's emotional well-being.

This is a reflection of students not considering the residual effect negative responses to personal experiences shared, have on emotions, and the level to which the impact may be. Students have become "comfortable" sharing without considering the level of trust they have with their social media "friends" and the public, in general. Students who take into consideration how much they "trust" others on a social media platform are less likely to put themselves in a difficult position. The irony is students have become more willing to share personal stories openly on social media but are more reticent to do so with an adult in private.

One possible reason for the varying trust levels is that it may be easier for students to avoid any awkwardness that may come about as a result of face-to-face exchanges. It has been suggested that many students choose to use text messaging rather than voice calling in order to avoid any awkward moments of silence that occur during spoken conversations. The result of this change in communication preferences is a generation finding greater social-emotional challenges than previous ones.

Finding a means to have a deep, intimate conversation with a student face to face and using such times to help the student identify and embrace their feelings for the purpose of helping them grow socially and emotionally is the challenge teachers find themselves confronting. The more a teacher is able to engage with a student in conversations about their feelings, the more opportunity there is to grow student understanding of the varying intensity levels of emotions.

As a part of the labeling process and understanding the varying levels of intensity of emotions, teachers are encouraged to expand their understanding

Table 9.1   Levels of Emotions

	Happy	Depressed	Fear	Anger	Hurt
		Vocabulary			
Intense	Ecstatic	Dejected	Desperate	Belligerent	Abused
	Enthusiastic	Despondent	Distressed	Fuming	Crushed
	Euphoric	Grieved	Intimidated	Heated	Devastated
	Excited	Hopeless	Terrified	Infuriated	Rejected
Moderate	Cheerful	Awful	Afraid	Aggravated	Belittled
	Delighted	Discouraged	Anxious	Irritated	Criticized
	Happy	Miserable	Fearful	Spiteful	Resentful
	Jovial	Upset	Nervous	Ticked Off	Troubled
Dull	Content/Satisfied	Disappointed	Apprehensive	Bothered	Annoyed
	Fine	Down	Cautious	Indignant	Ignored
	Glad	Uncomfortable	Uneasy	Irked	Left Out
	Pleased	Unhappy	Worried	Offended	Put Down

of this complexity by familiarizing themselves with lists of emotions. A Google search of "list of emotions" generates almost 1,69000,000 responses. Next is an example of a short chart, but there are those that are much more detailed (table 9.1).

How Does Helping Label Compare with Affect Labeling

Research has shown that simply helping a student label an emotion can help him or her respond more readily from a disturbing or troubling event. In a brain imaging study conducted by psychologists at the University of California, Los Angeles (UCLA) (2007), researchers found that verbalizing one's feelings reduces the impact of negative feelings or specifically, the emotion feels less intense. In other words, being able to identify and name an emotion can have a positive impact on how we feel.

The idea of putting words to feelings is not a new construct. For over a century, talk therapy has used the notion that simply talking about how one feels can make one feel better. Recently, this idea has been the target of a myriad of studies in education, psychology, child development, and other social science fields. Such studies refer to the practice of naming our emotions as "affect labeling." However, before we go any further, it is important to note that there is a key difference between the goal of affect labeling therapy and what we propose in this chapter. Regardless, labeling emotions is an important step toward effectively understanding them and dealing with them in a positive manner.

The key difference between "affect labeling" and "helping label" is this: affect labeling is a therapeutic construct that uses the process of talking about emotions as an implicit means of regulating emotions. This is quite different from the goal of helping label the emotion. Helping a student label a feeling is a step in the *emotion coaching* process used to put words to a specific feeling. It is a learning tool aimed at helping the student grow in emotional intelligence. Both may have the same desired outcome eventually, however, affect labeling is more narrow in scope than helping the student understand one's feelings. Thus, while a benefit beyond identifying the emotion and its level of intensity exists (e.g., helping de-escalate the student through lessening the intensity of the emotion), it should be viewed only as a step in the *emotion coaching* process and not as a means to an end in and of itself.

There is a sense of obligation to reiterate that when using the term "affect labeling," we are referring to an exercise in emotional regulation. The *emotion coaching* habit is referred to as "helping label." While clearly different constructs, there is overlap in benefits. And, since affect labeling has been demonstrated to produce positive unique benefits in and of itself, it obligates us to delve a little deeper into the matter in order to accentuate the importance of the labeling habit during the *emotion coaching* process.

The focus on affect labeling thus far has been on the benefits it has on regulating emotions. As such, the question that must be asked is: "What are the regulatory effects of the process?" Research on the regulatory effects of affect labeling on emotions is complex and mixed. One reason any research on the practice is complex is because such studies are focused on an unobservable variable—feelings. As such, scientists have had to rely on brain imaging and skin conductance response measures to get an accurate sense of what is occurring in the body as a result of the process. By doing so, researchers have been able to quantify some of the emotional regulatory effects of the process, most notably reduced activity in the amygdala (see the UCLA study referred to previously), and a lower skin conductance response to frightening stimuli (Torre and Lieberman, 2018).

This is all well said and done, but what does it mean for the teacher? Not a whole lot at face value. The main thing for the teacher to understand is that the process of helping the student label an emotion does have a direct physical benefit that correlates with an emotional one. As the student identifies the emotion, the body responds in a manner that helps lessen the impact of the emotion. In simpler terms, the process of labeling the emotion helps serve in de-escalating the intensity of the response. However, this is where a divide occurs between affect labeling and *emotion coaching*.

Emotion coaching is about growing emotionally intelligent students, moving beyond simply regulating one's emotions. First and foremost, labeling the emotion helps the student eliminate any uncertainty about the way they feel. It begins the process of understanding the impact one's feelings have on their own behaviors. The student is able to cognitively understand their feelings prior to reacting to them in an inappropriate way. The ability to specify the emotion allows the student to process the situation and respond with a more positive social behavior.

A second benefit of labeling emotions is that it forces the student to become more reflective. In order to name an emotion, the student must first pinpoint the feeling, which requires that they take time to reflect. According to research conducted by Baer, Smith, and Allen (2004), reflecting on one's own experiences, especially emotional ones, allows one to become more aware of the present moment. It is common for students to be aware of their surroundings during times in which negative emotions are high. As the student processes such experiences, they become even more aware. As such, teachers may find that there are those students who seem to be more aware than others are during negative experiences. These are the students who are further along the EQ scale than others.

SUMMARY

Teachers who seek to help students grow emotionally intelligent recognize the importance of the "helping label" habit. In fact, they understand the significance of broadening the student's and their own vocabulary of emotions. They desire for the student to understand the words they associate with specific emotions in order to understand the different intensity levels of the emotions. They are reflective teachers and encourage their students to be as well. And most importantly, they establish a rapport with their students that allows students to feel free to be open and honest with them. Being able to determine and label an emotion happens most easily when there is a strong bond between teacher and student.

For many students, talking about feelings or having to discuss things that upset them is not a pleasant experience. Most often, these are students who have been raised to believe emotions need to be suppressed. For some, that is a result of the home environment in which they were raised. For others, it was the organizational rules of the school. Whether intentional or unintentional, the result for the student is a stunted growth in emotional intelligence. That is why the teacher's ability to not only effectively address emotional situations but also create an environment where students feel safe to express emotions is important. In fact, it is a key leadership skill.

As teachers, we need to be cognizant that during each encounter we have with students, we send an emotional signal. These signals have an impact on them. As such, the more adept we are at managing the signals we send, the more positive the social environment we establish in the classroom is. The stronger our EQ, the better our social-emotional skills, and the better our students feel around us. The better the students feel with us, the more willing they will be to open up. The more a student is willing to share, the easier it becomes in helping them label and understand their feelings and support their growth in emotional intelligence.

Chapter 10

Habit 5

Problem-Solving

INTRODUCTION

So now that we have helped the student label the emotion, what is next? The time has come to focus on problem-solving skills. Here is where you get to the heart of the matter, helping the student understand what is inappropriate and what is appropriate in terms of behaviors. As expressed earlier in this book, one of the desired outcomes in growing emotionally intelligent students is the ability to respond with positive behaviors to negative emotions.

Remember, the *emotion coaching* process is designed to cultivate positive EQ growth and helps students develop a high self-esteem and sense of self-compassion in order to be more confident facing daily challenges and solving personal problems. The ability to problem-solve is a key component in that. And, the key to problem-solving starts with helping the student understand the importance of setting limits on how we respond to our emotions. This chapter focuses on the importance of how establishing boundaries and giving students choices go hand and hand with teaching students important problem-solving skills (figure 10.1).

> Boundaries define us. They define what is me and what is not me. A boundary shows me where I end and someone else begins, leading me to a sense of ownership. Knowing what I am to own and take responsibility for gives me freedom.—*Henry Cloud*

First Things First: Setting Limits

You are probably thinking, I am a teacher, I know the importance of setting limits and establishing boundaries. That is true. The focus here is on helping the

Teaching and building trust   *Awareness of emotions*

EMOTION COACHING:

WHAT IS IT?

Problem Solving   *Helping label*   *Empathy*

Figure 10.1.   The Five Habits: Problem-solving.

student distinguish the difference of behaviors with negative consequences from those with positive ones. This helps assist the student in setting limits on his responses to emotions. It is important to note this step may be easier to accomplish for a teacher working with secondary students than with younger ones. If the student is much younger, the adult may have to help set the parameters.

To help get a better understanding of the focus here, let's refer back to an example utilized throughout this book, that of a student who most often responded to feelings of anger by punching things. The following is one of the early discourses between the administrator and the student. As you may recall, the student had a habit of punching things when he was angered. In general, this aggression was taken out on material things such as walls and lockers. It is important to note that it was rare that he actually ever got into a physical altercation with another student.

During the *coaching* process, dialogue arose on problems associated with his punching behaviors. First and foremost, the issue of well-being was discussed. This topic arose as a result of one such angry outburst in which the student had punched a wall. On that specific occasion, he broke his hand and needed medical attention. That led to the second consequence of his punching behaviors, the monetary impact on him. On a number of occasions, the student found himself having to compensate the school for the repair or replacement of damaged items.

In this case, it was easy for the educator to be aware of the negative consequences of the student's behavior. And suffice it to say, the student was aware as well. As such, one would think setting limits would be easy—do not punch people and things, especially things that can break one's hand. However, the setting limits step of the process does not refer directly to the negative behavior, the negative behavior needs to be completely replaced with a positive one.

Setting limits refers to helping the student think through possible solutions to the problem. As you will see, it is imperative that the educator be keenly aware of positive and negative consequences of each possibility the student may suggest. This knowledge will help in setting limits and play an important role in the problem-solving process. And you will see that semantics may play a role. Let us return to the previous example for further clarification. Here is what the dialogue sounded like during the processing phase:

Student: "I do not understand why I keep being sent to the office. I did not hit anyone."
Educator: "My goal is to try and help you find more socially appropriate ways to express your anger."
Student: "That is how we express our anger in my neighborhood. It is considered socially appropriate there."
Educator: "Let's think in terms of the broader society. What are some alternative ways you could respond to anger without punching a wall or person?"
Student: "You can keep a punching bag in your office and allow me, and other students, to use it when we get angry and aggressive."

On the surface, the idea may seem like a reasonable alternative; it addresses two issues associated with his problem behavior: (1) allowing him to get his aggression out; and (2) allowing it to happen in a safe manner. We may recall though, that the goal of potential solutions is to help the student eliminate the problem behavior, not just the consequences of it. Further consideration of this suggestion reveals that the inappropriate behavior is not addressed. It is at this point that the educator needs to help the student set limits around any solution that involves punching, even if it sounds reasonable. As such, the conversation continued as follows:

Educator: "That seems like a reasonable recommendation. How would it help?"
Student: "Well, I would be able to get my aggression out in a safe manner. I would not hurt myself or anyone else, or break anything."
Educator: "True. But do you think it is the best way to express your anger?"
Student: "No. I probably should not be punching at all."
Educator: "True. So we need to come up with ideas that avoid that sort of behavior."

By doing so, the teacher is helping the student set limits that will help narrow down possible solutions to those that will best help achieve the overall goal.

Another key part of the process is to help the student understand why the limits are important even if the solution appears to help address the issue. In this circumstance, the following questions could be asked to help the student get a better understanding:

"What will you do when the punching bag is not available?"
"What will you do when you are not at school?"

"How will this help in the workplace, will you ask future employers to keep a
    punching bag accessible?"

Of course, this is the type of conversation a teacher who works with older
students can have. What about those of us who work with younger elementary
students?

Teachers who work with younger students will want to play a more active
role in establishing the limits with the student. Let's consider a similar case
scenario to the high school student who punches. In this scenario, an elementary school teacher is working with a young student who has a habit of hitting
classmates or breaking things when angry. Rather than asking questions that
cause the student to reflect on their behavior and come up with limitations, the
teacher will want to be more direct in guiding them. For example, a conversation may look like the following:

Teacher: "I saw you hit your friend. Were you mad at him?"
Student: "Yeah. He was not being nice to me."
Teacher: "I can understand why you would be mad, but do you think hitting him
    is right?"
Student: (Hopefully answers) "No. It is not good to hit others. But he made me
    mad."
Teacher: "I can see that. But remember how we learned it is not good to hit others?"
Students: "Yeah, I know I shouldn't get mad."
Teacher: "It is okay to get mad. It is not okay to hit others as a result. Can you
    think of other ways you could let someone know you are mad without hitting
    them, or yelling at them?"

In this conversation, the teacher has adeptly achieved three objectives in the
emotion coaching process: (1) she has reinforced with the student that the
emotion is not the problem, the behavior is; (2) she has effectively set limits
on behaviors the student may consider; and (3) she has reminded the student
of positive classroom behaviors that have been established.

The previous examples were provided simply to serve as a reminder of
the importance of knowing the desired outcome of the process and taking
the time to discuss the pros and cons of each suggested alternative behavior.
Again, the key to the process is to convey the message that feelings are not
the problem, inappropriate responses are, and so better methods of handling
these emotions are necessary.

Next Steps: Identifying Goals

After helping the student set limits on behaviors, have the student identify
goals around problem-solving (Gottman, 1997). In the previous examples,
goals were mentioned but those were established by the teacher and focused

on stopping the inappropriate behavior. Here we want the student to expand on that by identifying what may be the source of the emotion and what it is the student wants to accomplish. Remember, the goal is growth in emotional intelligence. Thus, to stop punching is not the ultimate goal.

Refer back to the previous two examples. We know with the elementary student that he was mad because his friend was not being nice to him. That information was not given regarding the high school student. In the high school case, he had been angered by a comment made by another student in one of his classes. Thus, the question that needed to be asked was "what was the reason for his punching?" Was it a means for releasing his anger? Or was it a desire to actually hurt someone?

Since the answer is probably a little of both, one could ask: "What difference does it make?" Remember, the focus of this habit is on helping the student identify goals. Goals focused on helping the student grow in emotional intelligence. In both examples, there are two issues at play: (1) how to express anger in healthy and more positive manners; and (2) how to confront someone appropriately and constructively when angered. At face value, they seem like one and the same. However, consider that these days' students are often taught to take deep breaths and walk away from the situation. This helps the student redirect the anger for now, but does not assist him in resolving his conflict with the other student.

Most often, the student will not recognize the two separate issues at play here: managing one's anger and resolving conflict. They are more likely to focus on the issue of punching/hitting solely. This is due to the reality that, most often, the issue will be the focus of the discipline and any dialogue around it. The matter of conflict resolution is not entirely dismissed by schools, most have some sort of conflict resolution meeting between the combatants. However, the focus of the majority of these meetings is on bringing about peace between two combatants, not on the individual emotional growth of each.

Hence, when identifying goals with the student, both issues will need to be introduced during the dialogue between teacher and student. It is important to note that, depending on the maturity of the student, it may be necessary to set one goal at a time. Dealing constructively with the other person could be a goal set for a later date. One caveat needs mentioning: sometimes it is necessary to delay meeting with the other student as a means for de-escalating emotions. Depending on the intensity level of the emotion, the student may need time to process in a quiet place. In such instances, it is beneficial for the teacher to have a written sheet of questions for the student to reflect on in solitude.

Consider arranging a quiet, safe place for the student to complete a ready-made questionnaire that may include the following questions:

- How are you feeling right now?
- What words best describe how you were feeling at the time of the incident?
- Did you do something considered inappropriate behavior?
- If so, what was the behavior?
- What and how did it happen?
- Why did it happen?
- What was your responsibility?
- What was running through your mind at the time?
- If it were possible to change things, what would you do differently?

One thing to notice about the suggested questions is that they are aimed at helping the student delineate between their behaviors and their emotions. Specifically, the focus is meant to be on the behavior being inappropriate, not the emotion. They are designed to get the student thinking in terms of alternative behaviors rather than hiding the emotion.

The questionnaire serves as a means for opening up the student to dialogue. After the student has completed the questionnaire, and their emotions have settled down, the teacher can process the events and behaviors with the student. The questionnaire should also serve as a tool that affords the student the opportunity to lead the discussion. By reading the student's answers prior to any discussion, the teacher is better able to understand the student's feelings at the time and thoughts about the circumstances. This allows the teacher to come to the dialogue better prepared.

After discussing the answers to the questionnaire with the student, the teacher may consider asking other probing questions:

- What actions could you take to make circumstances right again?
- Is there something going on in your life that I do not know about that is making things tough on you right now?

It may also be good to circle around again to the student's feelings. After dialoguing with the student, verbally ask how they are feeling to gauge the impact that conversing about the situation may have had on them. And as always, ask the student if there is anyone else they would like to talk to, someone they would feel more comfortable sharing openly with. This is the time where egos must be set aside. While you have built a trusting relationship with the student, there just may be someone else at the school with whom they would like to share.

Don't forget to also circle back to the reason for this step, identifying goals. The purpose of this process is to help the student identify goals aimed at responding to their feelings with positive behaviors. Remember, we want to recognize the source of the emotion and what it is he or she wants to accomplish. The goal is growth in emotional intelligence. As such, just stating they want to stop the inappropriate behavior falls short of the desired outcome in this step.

This is where *emotion coaching* differs from more traditional models for addressing negative student behaviors. In traditional models, there is limited dialogue. As such, a timeline of events will most often look like this: stimulating event occurs -> problem behavior occurs -> adult intervention (student meets with administrator/dean of discipline) -> consequence assigned. The *emotion coaching* flow is more like: stimulating event occurs -> problem behavior occurs -> adult intervention (remove the student to a quiet place) -> student completes questionnaire or some intervention to de-escalate the emotion -> adult dialogue including identifying goals -> interventions and appropriate consequences as necessary.

It needs to be noted here that the *emotion coaching* process is a tool to help student growth in emotional intelligence. It does not circumvent consequences for correcting problem behaviors. It does, however, assist in determining logical consequences for the misbehavior. You may recall the discussion around the idea of logical consequences that occurred earlier in this book. Too often school discipline codes rest on consequences that are poorly justified and fail to distinguish the difference between student behaviors associated with a low EQ (e.g., outbursts of frustration; hyperactivity not associated with ADHD) and behaviors associated with a lack in character development (e.g., stealing, lying, and vandalism).

This dichotomy is why identifying goals is such a prominent step in the process. The goal is to change from a focus on consequences and simple obedience to the rules, to helping the student redirect problem behaviors by growing in emotional intelligence. This requires schools to move beyond a focus on simply creating a safe and orderly environment to growing emotionally intelligent students. If schools are to take seriously the emotional development of students, as a component of improving positive interpersonal skills, their approach to discipline should become a conduit for growth in social-emotional intelligence. Including students in the process of identifying personal growth goals is a key component.

Problem-Solving: Finding a Positive Solution

Now that limits on behaviors have been set and the student has identified goals, the time has come to problem-solve (Gottman, 1997). In this phase, the teacher is simply trying to get the student to think of potential solutions. During this phase of the process, it may be necessary to remind the student of any limits on behaviors that have been established and of the identified goals. As was the case with the earlier steps of this phase, it may be necessary for teachers working with younger students to offer potential ideas. Teachers with older students will want to guide but try their best to have the student come up with a list of solutions.

A key component of this step is reiterating the source of the emotion and what it is they want to accomplish. Referring back to our example, the young man was angered by a comment made by another student in one of his classes. The student in that case identified two goals: releasing anger in a positive manner and confronting others in a non-confrontational way. To simplify the process, the focus would be on one goal at a time. As such, the student was directed to concentrate on potential actions for releasing anger in a more positive manner, without the need to punch anything, rather than how to confront the other person constructively. Dealing constructively with the other person would be addressed at a later time.

One caveat, sometimes, depending on the emotion and the goal, there may not be an immediate solution in sight. In such cases, the student may just need a little more direction. The teacher may need to encourage the student through the use of role-play or case scenarios. Gottman suggests presenting two solutions, a "wrong" one and a "right" one. After presenting each scenario, allow the student to talk about each one and present what was good and what was bad. This approach to problem-solving is more often needed when working with younger children.

Older students should simply be challenged to present a list of ideas, as many as they can think of without worrying about which ones may be good and which ones, bad, at this point. Still, it is good practice for the teacher to use this opportunity to help the student frame their thinking in relation to identified goals and positive behaviors. Think back to our earlier example about punching. Since one goal was to stop punching, the student was reminded to think of solutions that did not involve punching. Additionally, the student was encouraged to think in terms of behaviors that may help him develop patience, show compassion or kindness, and respect.

At first, this may be difficult for the student. In such cases, the educator may offer ideas or suggestions, such as "I have heard that some people in that situation have done the following." Once again, referring back to our earlier example of the younger student who hit a friend because they were not being nice. A conversation around possible solutions could look like this:

Teacher: "I see he made you upset by what he said. Instead of hitting him, is there another way you could have responded that you can think of?"
Student: "No."
Teacher: "Why is that?"
Student: "I don't know. Hitting him lets him know I am mad."

Teacher: "But we agreed hitting is not a nice thing to do. Besides, do you remember what you identified as your goal?"

Student: "Yes. To stop hitting people when I get mad."

Teacher: "So, what is a different way you could have responded?"

Student: "I don't know."

The teacher at this point has two options: (1) he can suggest that they visit this idea at a later time to give him time to think about alternative behaviors; or (2) he can respond with something like the following:

Teacher: "If we cannot come up with alternatives and you keep hitting other students, you will keep getting into trouble. And consequences may get harsher. You know, I have heard other children say that when they get mad they simply tell the other person they made them mad. Is that something you think might work for you?" Depending on the student's response, the teacher could encourage the student to think of other responses, or encourage him to begin practicing this strategy for now. The important thing is that the teacher frame the discussion in terms of identified goals and takes time to talk about the consequences of not having an alternative.

In terms of the older student, once a list of possible solutions has been made, the teacher should help the student process the solution that is most suitable (Gottman, 1997), framing the solution in terms of the pros and cons of the behavior and how it leads to meeting the identified goals. Always remember to discuss the ramifications of all possible solutions; for example, using a punching bag still promotes punching.

As with younger students, on occasion, older students prefer to not come up with a solution; discuss ramifications of not having one. In the aforementioned example regarding the high school student, the ramifications are obvious and not so good for the student: monetary losses, medical expenses, and arthritis later in life. The key is to get the student to think beyond the current situation and toward a more long-term perspective. Because children and adolescents notoriously have difficulty delaying immediate gratification, teachers need to help students learn to think in terms of the long-term consequences of their behaviors, and situations such as these are excellent opportunities to do so.

Wrapping It All Up

Remember that the ultimate goal of this process is to help the student grow in emotional intelligence. The purpose is to help students learn to behave in ways that are considered good and to help them in framing their mindsets in a manner that is cognizant of the views of everyone who is impacted by behavior. As such, the teacher's focus is on helping students live beyond the constructs of rules and regulations and simply acting in a manner of obedience to them. Through the *emotion coaching* process, the student will come to understand and embrace their feelings with the added benefits of conducting themselves in pro-social manners.

The key in this whole process is for the teacher to not give into the temptation to fix the problem for the student, but rather to assist the student with reflection and discovery. In doing so, the teacher not only assists the student in determining the best methods for acting appropriately in the future but also assists them in growing emotionally stronger. It is important to remember that the student will move on from the teacher and school at some point, and must come to a point where they are comfortable with who they are and their ability to manage their own behaviors. Emotionally intelligent students are self-confident and compassionate and act in socially appropriate manners under any circumstance, without the constant guidance of an adult.

Growing emotionally intelligent students is not an easy venture. Teachers are challenged in a multitude of ways that have an impact on time and energy that can be put into such efforts. As discussed early on, one of the greatest challenges for teachers is found in the reality that school programs are limited in the amount of time with which they can work with students before they return to a larger society. If teachers are to be successful in their efforts of developing students' emotional intelligence, it will require efforts that extend beyond the school day and focus on giving individual students the tools, understanding and resolve needed to remain positive in an ever-challenging world.

References

BOOKS CITED

Arthur, J., Kristjansson, K., Harrison, T., Sanderse, W., and Wright, D. (2017). *Teaching character and virtues in schools*. Routledge.

Berkowitz, M. (2012). *You can't teach through a rat: And other epiphanies for educators*. Character Development Group, Inc.

Blankenstein, A. (2010). *Failure is not an option: 6 principles for making student success the only option*. Corwin Press.

Brown, B. (2018). *Dare to lead: Brave work. Tough conversations. Whole hearts.* Penguin Random House LLC.

Character Education Partnership (2005). *Creating A Caring School Community*. Washington, DC: Author.

Gardener, H. (1983). *Frames of mind: The theory of multiple intelligences*. Basic Books.

Gladwell, M. (2005). *Blink: The power of thinking without thinking*. Little, Brown and Company.

Goleman, D. (1995). *Emotional Intelligence*. Bantam Books.

Gottman, J. (1997). *Raising an emotionally intelligent child: The heart of parenting*. Simon and Schuster.

Hoffman, A. (2020). *Magic lessons: The prequel to practical magic*. Simon & Schuster.

Hylen, M. (2008). *The impact of a character education based interactive discipline program on at-risk student behavior in an alternative school*. ProQuest LLC.

Knight, J. (2015). *Better conversations: Coaching ourselves and each other to be more credible, caring, and connected*. Corwin Press.

Lencioni, P. (2012). *The advantage*. HarperCollins Publishers.

Lewis, M. (1993). Self-conscious emotions: Embarrassment, pride, shame and guilt. In M. Lewis and J. M. Haviland (Eds.), *Handbook of emotions* (pp. 563–573). Guilford Press.

Lickona, T. (1991). *Educating for character: How schools can teach respect and responsibility.* Bantam Books.

MacDonald, G. (2015) *The marquis of Lossie.* Jefferson Publication. [Original printing: 1877, Hurst and Blackett].

Ormrod, J. E. (2003). *Educational psychology: Developing learners* (4th edition). Pearson Education, Inc.

Payne, R. (1995). *A framework for understanding poverty: A cognitive approach.* aha! Process, Inc.

Skinner, B.F. (1971). *Beyond freedom and dignity.* Alfred Knopf, Inc.

Valkenburg, P.M., and Piotrowski, J.T. (2017). *Plugged in: How media attract and affect youth.* Yale University Press.

Vincent, P. (2005). *Restoring school civility: Creating a caring, responsible, and productive school.* Character Development Group, Inc.

Vincent, P., and Grove, D. (2013). *Relationships + Rules + Routines = Results: A common sense approach.* Character Development Group, Inc.

Wagner, T., and McGee, J. (2016). *Re/engage.* Marriage workshop.

Waltz, G.R., and Bleuer, J.C. (1992). *Student self-esteem: A vital element of school success. Volume 1.* Counseling and Personal Services.

Warner, M., and Coursey, C. (2019). *The 4 habits of joy-filled marriages.* Moody Publishers.

Yerkovich, M., and Yerkovich, K. (2017). *How we love.* WaterBrook.

Zimmer, B. (2003). *Reflections for tending the sacred garden: Embracing the art of slowing down.* iUniverse, Inc.

ARTICLES CITED

Attard, A. (2020). *Repressing emotions: 10 ways to reduce emotional avoidance.* Downloaded from https://positivepsychology.com/positive-emotions/

Baer, R. Smith, G., and Allen, K. (2004). *Assessment of mindfulness by self-report: The Kentucky inventory of mindfulness skills.* Retrieved from https://www.researchgate.net/publication/8355105_Assessment_of_Mindfulness_by_Self-Report_The_Kentucky_Inventory_of_Mindfulness_Skills

Berkowitz, M. (2012b). *Educating for a just and caring democratic society: Foundations of effective school reform.* Paper presentation for the Jubilee Centre for Character and Virtues conference titled "Character and Public Policy: Educating for an Ethical Life" on 14th - 15th December 2012. Retrieved May 28, 2015, http://www.jubileecentre.ac.uk/userfiles/jubileecentre/pdf/conference-papers/BerkowitzM-Educating-for-a-Just-andCaringDemocraticSociety.pdf

Bloom, L., and Bloom, C. (2019). *Self-trust and how to build it.* Downloaded from https://www.psychologytoday.com/us/blog/stronger-the-broken-places/201909/self-trust-and-how-build-it

Bonier, A. (2018). *7 Ways to build trust in a relationship.* Downloaded from https://www.psychologytoday.com/us/blog/friendship-20/201812/7-ways-build-trust-in-relationship.

Chambers, E., Hylen, M., Schreiber, J., and Asner-Self, K. (2005). *At-risk middle school students' perspective of school climate and its impact on achievement.* Presentation at the annual meeting for the American Educational Research Association, Montreal, QC.

Chambers, E.A., Hylen, M., and Schreiber, J.B. (2006). Achievement and at-risk middle school students' perspectives of academic support. *Journal of Research in Character Education,* 4, 33–46.

Craig, H. (2020) *10 ways to build trust in a relationship.* Downloaded from https://positivepsychology.com/build-trust/

Davies, A. (2010). *A brief introduction to dissociation.* Retrieved from https://www.aipc.net.au/articles/a-brief-introduction-to-dissociation/

Doyle, L., and Doyle, P. (2003). Building schools as caring communities: Why, what, and how? *The Clearing House,* 76, 259–261.

Elkind, D., and Sweet, F. (2004). *How to do character education.* Retrieved June 11, 2015, from http://www.goodcharacter.com/Article_4.html.

Fries, A. W., Ziegler, T., Kurian, J., Jacoris, S., and Pollak, S. (2005). Early experience in humans is associated with changes in neuropeptides critical for regulating social behavior. *Proceedings of the National Academy of Sciences of the United States of America,* 102, 17237–17240.

Gregory, A., and Ripski, M.B. (2008). Adolescent trust in teachers: Implications for behavior in the high school classroom. *School Psychology Review,* 37(3), 337–353. doi: 10.1080/02796015.2008.12087881

Hansen, J. (2014). *Relationship between teacher perception of positive behavior interventions support and the implementation process.* Doctoral dissertation, The University of Southern Mississippi. Available from ProQuest Dissertations and Theses database (UMI No. 3584518).

Jeffrey, S. (n.d.). *Repressed emotions: A guide to understanding feelings hidden within us.* Downloaded from https://scottjeffrey.com/repressed-emotions/#2_Suppressing_the_Emotion

Jehn, K., Chadwick, C., and Thatcher, S. (1997). *To agree or not agree: The effects of value congruence, individual demographic dissimilarity, and conflict on workgroup outcomes.* Retrieved from https://psycnet.apa.org/record/1997-39065-001

Mitchell, R., Kensler, L., and Tschannen-Moran, M. (2018). Student trust in teachers and student perceptions of safety: Positive school predictors of student identification with school. *International journal of leadership in Education,* 21(2), 135–154. doi: 10.1080/13603124.2016.1157211

Salavoy, P., and Mayer, JD. (1990). Emotional intelligence. *Imagination, Cognition and Personality,* 9(3), 185–211.

Shemla, M., Meyer, B., Greer L., and Jehn, K. (2016). A review of perceived diversity in teams: Does how members perceive their team's composition affect team processes and outcomes? *Journal of Organizational Behavior,* 37, 89–106.

Taylor, S. (2015). *Understanding empathy: Shallow and deep empathy.* Downloaded from https://www.psychologytoday.com/us/blog/out-the-darkness/201509/understanding-empathy

References

Torre, J., and Lieberman, M. (2018). Putting feelings into words: Affect labeling as implicit emotion regulation. *Emotion Review*, 10(2), 116–124. doi: 10.1177/17 54073917742706

University of California - Los Angeles. (2007, June 22). Putting feelings into words produces therapeutic effects in the brain. *ScienceDaily*. Retrieved from www.sciencedaily.com/releases/2007/06/070622090727.htm

Van Maele, D., and Van Houtte, M. (2011). The quality of school life: Teacher student trust relationships and the organizational school context. *Social Indicators Research*, 100, 85–100. doi:10.1007/s11205-010-9605-8

Vodicka, D. (2006). The four elements of trust. *Principal Leadership*, 7(3), 27–30.

Whitted, K. (2011). Understanding how social and emotional skill deficits contribute to school failure. *Preventing School Failure,* 55, 10–16.

Wismer Fries, A.B., Ziegler, T.E., Kurian, J.R., Jacoris, S., and Pollack, S.D. (2005). Early experience in humans is associated with changes in neuropeptides for regulating behavior. *PNAS*, 102(47), 17327–17240.

WEBSITES CITED

ACCIPIO: www.accipio.com

BBC Broadcaster: www.bbc.co.uk

Coalition for Children: www.safechild.org

Positive Psychology.com: www.positivepsychology.com

Restorative Justice Colorado: www.rjcolorado.org

The Roots of Educational Theory: www.educationalroots.weebly.com

The School of Life: www.theschooloflife.com

Wikipedia: www.en.wikipedia.org

About the Author

Michael G. Hylen serves as the Coordinator of Doctoral Studies in education and Associate Professor of Graduate Studies at Southern Wesleyan University in South Carolina. He has also served as a professor in the education departments at Louisiana State University Shreveport and Asbury University in Wilmore, Kentucky. Prior to joining the higher education ranks, he enjoyed a twenty-five-year career as a K–12 educator, both as a teacher and an administrator.

His most extensive work was as an alternative high school principal for students who struggled in traditional school settings, often due to social-emotional challenges. He has earned PhD from the University of Missouri St. Louis with a specific emphasis on at-risk students and problem behaviors. It was due to the role of alternative school principal that he became more interested in social emotional learning and emotional intelligence.

Michael remains actively involved in K–12 education by speaking at conferences and providing professional development on emotional intelligence. He has had the privilege of doing so on the local, national, and international levels.